THEMES ON DISPLAY
for early years

Seasonal
Displays

GEORGIE BEASLEY
AND
ANN MOBERLEY

AUTHORS GEORGIE BEASLEY AND ANN MOBERLEY

EDITOR SUSAN HOWARD

ASSISTANT EDITORS LESLEY SUDLOW AND SALLY GRAY

SERIES DESIGNER LYNNE JOESBURY

DESIGNER MARK UDALL

ILLUSTRATIONS CATHY HUGHES

PHOTOGRAPHS MARTYN CHILLMAID

With thanks to Miss Andrea Conroy, Nursery Nurse NNEB, who helped with all the displays and to all the parents and children at Moons Moat First School, Redditch.

Designed using Adobe Pagemaker

Published by Scholastic Ltd, Villiers House, Clarendon Avenue, Leamington Spa, Warwickshire CV32 5PR
Text © Georgie Beasley and Ann Moberley

© 2000 Scholastic Ltd

1 2 3 4 5 6 7 8 9 0   0 1 2 3 4 5 6 7 8 9

British Library Cataloguing-in-Publication Data
A catalogue record for this book is available from the British Library.

ISBN 0-439-01737-8

Contents

THEMES ON DISPLAY for early years

THEMES ON DISPLAY for early years

Introduction

The importance of display

Displays are an important part of all early years settings. They provide an opportunity to celebrate children's work by providing a stimulating environment that can spark interest and inspire an enthusiasm for learning. *Themes on Display – Seasons* aims to provide advice and support to all early years educators to enable them to deliver the topic of Seasons through display.

The displays in this book can be used as starting points for the organization of structured play activities through which very young children learn best. Each display combines interactive activity with the children's own work. Some are intended to be used as instant displays to inspire interest for a new topic and all of the displays provide opportunities for cross-curricular learning.

Each chapter of displays is planned to be produced over a half-term and is organized so that all children, including those who attend the group part-time, can become involved in its production.

Themes on Display – Seasons contains five chapters – four covering the four seasons and a fifth which provides opportunities to develop the strands of weather, animal and plantlife and the months of the year. Continuous displays throughout the book provide opportunities for children to consider the things in the world around them which stay the same and those which change throughout the year. Each chapter contains a display which either celebrates a major Christian festival or a personal event such as birthdays. The displays in the chapter entitled 'The seasons' are ongoing and give a good opportunity to observe changes in the weather and plant life over the year. Additions can be made in response to the children's observations and your setting's religious make-up.

In Chapter 1, 'The seasons', children have the opportunity to consider the similarities, differences and changes which occur during and between seasons. The strands of weather, tree

Introduction

THEMES ON DISPLAY for early years

and other plantlife and the needs of animals are considered. There is also an opportunity to learn about the things that stay the same such as evergreen plants, birthdays and the names and order of the months.

Chapter 2 looks at 'Spring', the season of new life. The children are given the opportunity to consider not only new life when things begin to grow again, but also the activities in which humans partake, such as spring-cleaning! The Easter festival is celebrated and the weather theme is further extended.

Chapter 3 explores 'Summer', focusing on many of the activities in which the children take part such as visits to the park, playing out in the lighter evenings and going on picnics. Growth is explored further through the investigation of summer flowers. Children are also taught the importance of protecting themselves from the sun's harmful rays.

'Autumn' is looked at in Chapter 4. There are a series of displays that celebrate this season's blaze of colour. Reds, oranges, yellows, browns and greens are brought together in many displays about the changing environment. Harvest is the festival celebrated in this season.

The final chapter covers 'Winter'. The weather theme is extended through displays about snow and frosty weather. The needs of birds are considered and the festival of Advent is celebrated.

Each chapter begins with a stimulus display to introduce the season and to stimulate the children's interest. This is followed by five interactive displays which extend the theme of the chapter, encouraging the children to consider all aspects of each season or strand and to ask questions and make suggestions to extend their learning.

Many of these displays are interactive and invite the children to handle the resources and sort items. Each chapter ends with a table-top display that allows the children to contribute their own ideas and help to set up the display. There are also further ideas for display tables that you may wish to use to extend the theme.

Colour photographs throughout the book show the displays in detail and provide guidance on how the techniques, materials and colours have been used for best effect.

The text gives clear guidance on how the displays were initiated and contains all the information needed for early years practitioners to reproduce the displays in any early years setting.

Using the book

Each display is divided into subheadings:

● Learning objective

Each display begins with a detailed and specific learning objective linked to seasonal aspects of the Knowledge and understanding area of learning. It states clearly what the children are expected to know at the completion of the display.

Particular attention is given to developing the children's respect for all living things and an awareness of environmental issues.

● What you need

A detailed list gives information on everything required for the production of the display. Specific guidance is given on the sizes and types of papers, fabrics and recycled materials, the range of colouring medium and any items, objects and collections used. Ideas for creating special effects, labels, borders and titles are also given. There is also guidance on the best ways of attaching

the elements of the display to the background. While the list of items needed for each display is comprehensive, it is also flexible. Substitute items for your own displays as appropriate.

● What to do

This section provides step-by-step guidance on creating each display. Clear information on the type of wall space or display surface is given. There are suggestions for ways of covering display boards or surfaces, and ideas for adding interest by using covered boxes of different heights. Techniques are explained in detail and advice is given on suitable materials to use. Advice on organizing the activities, resources, children and adult helpers is also given.

● Talk about

This section includes suggestions for key points to talk about during and after the production of the display. Particular ideas on the development of language and the early scientific skills associated

Introduction

with observation, particularly noticing similarities, differences and changes, are given. Health and safety issues are also covered and care should be taken to ensure the safety of the children at all times when carrying out any investigational work. Suggestions for questions to challenge and extend children's thinking are particularly useful. Many suggested activities involve similar firsthand learning opportunities and chances to extend the learning objective through additional activities related to the display are included.

● Home links

The establishment and maintenance of home links is vital and this section includes suggestions on practical ways to involve children's parents and carers. These include suggestions for inviting parents and carers into your setting to help with specific skills such as cutting and modelling, asking them to contribute towards collections for the display, and suggesting activities to try at home with their children to reinforce the learning objective.

It is strongly suggested that you follow your setting's policy whenever you invite visitors in to talk and work with the children.

● Curriculum links

Each display includes suggestions for its use across the early years curriculum. The ideas extend and support work in Personal, social and emotional development, including religious education; Language and literacy, including the development of the role-play areas; Mathematical development with particular reference to numeracy; the other elements of Knowledge and understanding of the world including ICT, geography, history and D&T; Physical development, fine and gross motor skills; and Creative development including music, art and dance.

Many ideas can be used across several of the displays. For example, the development of the children's vocabulary skills as they explore the meanings and sounds of new words is suggested in the displays entitled 'Autumn leaves' on page 50 and 'Frosty weather' on page 68. Although this has not been specifically suggested for other displays, it can be applied just as effectively to many of them.

Information and communication technology

There are many opportunities to develop ICT links in this set of displays. Simple word-processing skills can be extended through the production of labels and sentences describing the content of the displays. Data-handling activities are highlighted in the 'Happy birthday!' display on page 14 and 'Weather forecast' on page 22. Encourage the children to operate a tape recorder by organizing a listening tape of different seasonal sound effects, such as rain falling or

birds singing, or let them listen to taped versions of stories. The children's mouse control skills can be developed by creating pictures to support displays using a suitable program, or by using specific programs such as 'Dress the Teddy' from *My World* (SEMERC).

Making the displays interactive

Plan to include as many interactive elements as possible in your display. This can be achieved through adding flaps to be lifted, items to be sorted and so on. These elements help to develop children's natural curiosity for exploration and investigation. Mathematical skills of counting and sequencing are developed effectively through the 'Christmas Advent tree' display on page 64, where the children are invited to count the days until Christmas by taking a decoration from the display and adding it to a decorated Christmas tree. Several displays such as 'Blossom trees' on page 25, encourage the development of creative skills by

inviting the children to mix paint to create the desired colours.

Involve the children in making items for the display both individually and in groups, and where possible, let them add their work to the display themselves. This helps to foster a sense of pride and ownership. Try to involve parents and carers in a number of ways. For example, you could suggest that they repeat or extend activities at home with their children; reinforce safety messages; come into the setting to help with different parts of the displays; and contribute items to the displays.

Planning displays

It is very important that display is included in your planning process. The environment of your setting plays a vital role in providing a stimulating, motivating and interesting learning environment for the children and can only be effective to learning if all staff who work in your setting develop its planned use. Identify opportunities for

Introduction

structured play activities to support children's learning beforehand, and plan to include opportunities to develop specific skills.

There is guidance on how to collect items, organize parents and carers to contribute and how to produce the stimulus displays to orchestrate the response that you want.

Stimulus displays

The stimulus displays at the beginning of each chapter can be put up in a few minutes and stored away for future use. It is a good idea to have a bank of such displays, which can be used at appropriate times to stimulate interest in a specific topic. Try to gather together a collection of items such as templates, examples of photocopiable sheets, labels and lettering, papers and drapes and a copy of your letter to parents to send out at the beginning of a new topic asking for their support and giving them valuable information on what the children will learn during the half-term.

Display tables

Select tables with shapes which complement the display. Choose tables that are the correct height and depth for the space you have available and which will show off the items in your collection to good effect. Look for fabrics and papers in interesting colours and textures to cover your table. Add a three-dimensional feel by arranging cardboard boxes or cylinders of different shapes and sizes, and covering the entire table with fabric before adding items to your table-top display.

Constructing aesthetic displays

Choose the colours and textures that you use for your displays carefully. Unusual materials with interesting textures can be used to great effect. For example, in the 'Magnificent trees' display on page 16, old, clean tights in different colours are stretched and stapled over the backing sheet to create trees in different seasons. The flexible material is extremely versatile and can be manipulated into a wide range of shapes and sizes. Similarly, in the display 'Cosy clothes' on page 61, real clothes have been used to dress the cut-out models of children.

Add three-dimensional effects with interesting techniques and objects. For example, you could add crumpled-up paper behind pictures before stapling to the background so that they stand out from the board, or add real items such as the bird cakes in the 'Winter birds' display on page 62. An old umbrella has also been used effectively in the 'March winds and April showers' display on page 30.

Mounting and framing

It is important to show children that their contributions are valued and this can be achieved through careful mounting and backing of individual pieces of work. Thoughtful use of colour, shape and texture and the imaginative arrangement of work are necessary to show it off to best effect. This helps to create additional interest and also motivates the children to interact with the display. Mount the children's pictures onto paper of a contrasting colour to provide a frame and to draw the eye to the picture. Use a glue stick on the outside edges and centre of the picture before sticking it to a piece of contrasting paper, leaving a border of approximately one centimetre all the way around.

Borders, titles and labels

Borders are an important part of any display, and there are ideas for creating effective borders which not only complete a display but also direct the observer's eye to the key parts. Make use of a variety of colours and varieties of paper such as scalloped card, coloured sugar paper, tissue and crêpe paper. Try different techniques, such as rippling the paper to create a wavy border or applying the border to certain parts of the display. On some of the displays in this book the border is continued in the display itself as a device to divide the display into sections.

Use the children's pictures, patterns and prints to create colourful borders. The 'January snow' display on page 66 and the 'Christmas Advent tree' on page 64 make use of children's sponge prints created using templates.

Emphasize titles by double mounting them on contrasting paper or by using different styles of type. Make movable labels that the children can place on appropriate parts of the display. Use folded card so that they are free-standing, or attach Velcro or Blu-Tack so that they can be repositioned.

Cutting and fixing

A guillotine is essential to make a clean cut along the edge of paper and also gives clear measurement support. Cut coloured paper into scalloped or shaped patterns using scissors. Interesting edges can also be produced by using pinking shears and other different-shaped scissors.

Useful resources

Many of the resources listed in the 'What you need' section are readily available in most early years settings, or can be obtained cheaply or free of charge. Look around your immediate environment to find fallen leaves, or examples of wildlife for the children to study. It is useful to have a few specialist items, such as:

- a sturdy gun stapler
- a small stapler
- sticky tape
- display pins
- guillotine strimmer
- glue sticks
- good quality rolls of backing paper which does not fade in the light and can be used to create interesting borders
- supplies of Cellophane, tissue and crêpe papers to add texture to displays
- a selection of textiles in a range of interesting patterns and bright colours including red, green, brown, orange,

Introduction

yellow and blue – old curtains are suitable
- a good quality PVA glue
- a range of paintbrushes and powder paint colours, which can be mixed to any required thickness
- a range of papers, fabrics and wool off-cuts sorted into colours and stored in suitable containers, for example plastic, transparent sweet jars are fine for wool
- good quality scissors for adult use
- collections of magazines, comics, mail-order catalogues and holiday brochures offering a wide range of pictures and colours for collage
- a range of cardboard boxes in different sizes and shapes, covered with different coloured paper and fabric.

Useful contacts
Many high street firms support early years settings and are only too pleased to contribute items for your displays. Approach printers for off-cuts of paper or cardboard – these are sometimes available free of charge if you are willing to collect them yourself.

Make use of local recycling centres, or ask around your local shops for display items that are no longer being used. Office stationers are often willing to donate out-of-date calendars or Christmas cards. Don't forget to make use of your local community, too. Put up a sign in the local library asking for donations of old Christmas cards, newspapers, fabric scraps and other collage materials.

The seasons

Changing seasons

Learning objective: to learn that there are four seasons in a year.

What you need
Orange backing paper; yellow card border; orange and yellow sugar paper; white card; sponge animal templates; the photocopiable sheet on page 73 enlarged to A3 size; a range of postcards and pictures depicting aspects of the four seasons; glue sticks; stapler.

What to do
Cover a display board with orange backing paper. Use the yellow card border to frame the area and divide it into four. Mount the enlarged poem in the centre of the display. Use sponge animal templates to print a decorated border around the poem if you wish. Double mount white card labels of 'spring', 'summer', 'autumn' and 'winter' onto orange and yellow sugar paper.

Gather the children together in front of the display and read the poem to them. Tell them that they are going to make a display of items and pictures of things that are found during each of the four seasons such as leaves, snowmen, baby animals and so on. Read the four labels to the children and then staple one label in each section. Make labels in the same way for the months, and the number of days in each month, and staple these in order across the tops of the appropriate sections on the board.

Finally, staple the postcards and pictures mounted onto yellow and orange sugar paper into the relevant sections, talking to the children as you do so. Add labels if you wish. Invite the children to bring additional pictures and items from home to add to the display.

Talk about
● Talk about the postcards and pictures. Invite the children to suggest where to place them on the display.
● Talk about the current season and find this on the display. Can the children recognize the season from the pictures?
● Add to the display during the year by talking about events as they happen.

Home links
● Invite carers and parents to help with seasonal events such as autumn and spring fairs and summer fêtes. Invite the children to paint pictures of these to add to the display.
● Ask parents to talk with their children about the seasons in which certain festivals occur. For example, talk about winter at Christmas, autumn at bonfire night, Holi in spring and so on.

From birthdays to Christmas trees, the display ideas in this chapter will help young children to think about the events, sights and sounds that they come into contact with throughout the year.

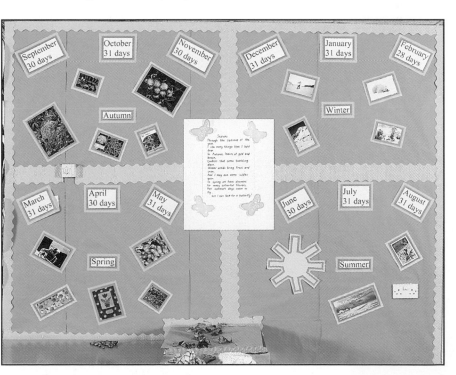

THEMES ON DISPLAY for early years

Interactive display

Happy birthday!

Learning objective: to begin to recognize the season in which own birthday falls.

What you need

A table; colourful backing paper; large piece of bright fabric; black sugar paper; white card; yellow card cut into small wedge shapes; black felt-tipped pen; coloured tissue paper; a model birthday cake; old birthday cards and wrapped 'presents'; coloured lettering; PVA glue; spreaders; stapler; balloons.

What to do

Cover a board with backing paper and divide the area into four sections with strips of black sugar paper. Add the title 'Birthdays' and label each section with the names of the four seasons, and the names of the months starting either with September or January.

Explain to the children that you are going to make a display to show the seasons and months in which their birthdays fall. Discuss who has a birthday coming up, or who has had one recently. Sing the song 'Happy Birthday to You'. Tell the children that they are going to make slices of birthday cake to place on the display to show when their birthdays are.

Organize the children into groups according to the months in which their birthdays fall. Give each child a yellow card wedge, and invite them to choose coloured tissue paper to stick onto the wedge to make 'icing'. Make labels for each of the children's names, mount them onto white card and stick them beneath the tissue paper icing. Invite the children to help you to staple their cake slices in the correct sections on the display.

Place a table in front of the display and cover it with fabric. Place a real or model birthday cake on the table and add birthday cards and wrapped

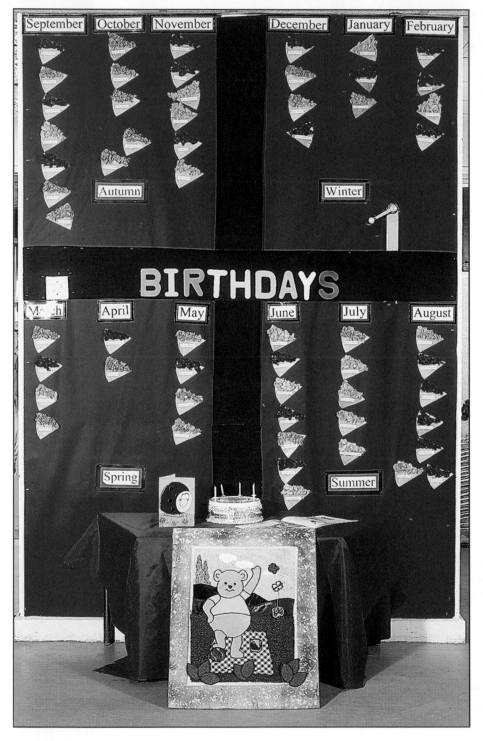

Using the display
Personal, social and emotional development
● Turn the role-play area into a party. Let the children organize their own games, devise some menus and set up a party table. Include colourful paper plates, dishes and cups and a range of pretend food items. Allow the children to operate a CD/tape player independently. NB Make sure that the children do not touch the mains electricity switches.

Language and literacy
● Read *Happy Birthday, Harvey Hare!* by Bernadette Watts (North-South Books).
● Ask the children to find their names on the display. Begin to teach them to write their name.
● Listen to rhymes about the seasons and months of the year, such as 'August', 'New Chicks', 'Flower Pots' from *A Year Full of Stories* by Georgie Adams and Selina Young (Dolphin) or *Out and About Through the Year* by Shirley Hughes (Walker Books).

Mathematical development
● Count the number of children who have birthdays in April, September, spring, winter and so on.
● Play counting games and learn rhymes about numbers up to 12, such as 'Ten Green Bottles', 'One Potato, Two Potato', 'Five Little Ducks' or 'Two Little Dicky Birds' all from *This Little Puffin...* compiled by Elizabeth Matterson (Puffin).

Knowledge and understanding of the world
● Ask a grandparent to come into the setting to talk about birthdays when they were young.

Physical development
● Play some party games such as 'Pass the Parcel' or 'Musical Chairs/Bumps/ Statues'.

Creative development
● Learn songs about the months of the year and the seasons such as 'The North Wind Doth Blow' from *Sing Hey Diddle Diddle* (A & C Black).

presents. When each of the children's birthdays come around, decorate the display with balloons.

Talk about
● Discuss the number of seasons. Ask the children how many months are there in each season.
● Talk about the names of the months and seasons. Which is the shortest? Which is the longest?
● Talk about the different ways in which birthdays are celebrated around the world.

Home links
● Ask parents and carers to come into your setting to help the children bake different kinds of birthday cakes from a range of cultures and made from different ingredients.
● Organize a birthday party for your group and ask parents to help by providing food and drink items and to join in with the party. Remember to check for any food allergies or special dietary requirements.

THEMES ON DISPLAY for early years

Magnificent trees

Learning objective: to learn that some trees change over the year and that this change takes place in the same season each year.

What you need

Green backing paper; white card labels; scalloped card; black marker pen; clean black, brown and flesh-coloured tights; red, yellow and orange tissue paper; paint in various colours; red, black, yellow and green sugar paper; green fabric; green wax crayons; scissors; PVA glue and spreaders; stapler.

What to do

Cover a display board with green backing paper. Use scalloped card to make a border and divide the area into four sections. Double mount labels of the four seasons onto green and red paper and staple one in each section.

Take the children around your setting or into the local area to look at the trees. Talk about the shape of the branches, the thickness of the trunk and the number, shape and colours of the leaves. Depending on the time of the year there may be fruits, nuts or blossom on the tree. On your return, tell the children that they are going to make four pictures of a tree to show the changes that occur during the year.

The four trees are made in the same way. Use brown tights for autumn, black for winter and flesh-coloured tights for spring and summer. Cut the legs of the tights into six to eight strips. Staple the tops of the tights to the bottom of each section then stretch them to make a trunk and branches, stapling into place as you go. Paint grey, black, turquoise and dark blue sky for autumn, winter, spring and summer respectively.

Using the display

Personal, social and emotional development
● Talk to the children about the importance of leaving trees and plants alone. Remind them that they should never pull off branches or pick leaves, fruits or seeds.

Language and literacy
● Focus on the sound 't'. Make a collection of objects and pictures beginning with 't'.
● Read *The Acorn's Story* by Valerie Greeley (Puffin) about how a tree grows and changes through the seasons.
● Play games listening to and recognizing the sound 't' when it appears in rhymes and poems.

Mathematical development
● Draw a simple outline of a tree and cut out ten leaf shapes. Invite the children to attach the leaves to the tree with Blu-Tack, counting together. Place all the leaves on the tree and remove them, counting back. Repeat, starting from different numbers.

Knowledge and understanding of the world
● Make a display of a tree trunk and branches. Record the changes in one tree in or near your setting by adding and removing leaves, blossom and fruit and by changing the colours of the leaves.

Physical development
● Develop cutting skills by providing leaf templates for the children to draw around and cut out.

Creative development
● Encourage the children to mix red and yellow paint to paint trees in autumn colours.
● Sing songs and action rhymes about trees through the seasons with the children such as 'I Had a Little Cherry Stone', 'Four Scarlet Berries' or 'Five Little Leaves' from *This Little Puffin...* compiled by Elizabeth Matterson (Puffin).

Organize the children into groups to make the leaves and blossom. For the spring tree, cut leaf shapes from green fabric and glue these in pairs to either side of the branches. Let the children finger-paint clusters of pink and white blossom on circles of red sugar paper. Staple these to the ends of the branches grouped into clusters. For the summer tree, add wax rubbings or real leaves. Make autumn leaves from red, orange and yellow tissue paper squares glued to different-sized yellow sugar paper leaf shapes. Staple these in groups around the ends of the branches. Leave the winter tree bare.

Talk about
● Talk about the different parts of the tree. Notice how the trunk and branches stay the same each season, but the leaves and blossom change.
● Look at the trees around the setting or local area. What season is it now? What do the trees look like?

Home links
● Ask parents and carers to accompany the children on walks around your setting or local area at different times of the year to look at the trees.
● Write to parents at the beginning of the year to tell them what you are doing. Ask them to point out the changes to the children as they happen, reminding them that some changes might occur during the holidays.

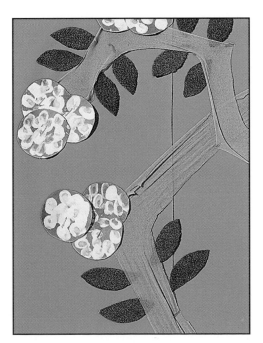

Animal life

Learning objective: to learn that different animals are seen at different times of the year and that some are seen all year round.

What you need

Backing paper; border card; white card; sugar paper in various colours; corrugated card; templates of an owl, hedgehog, blackbird, squirrel, mouse, robin, seagull, lambs, chicks, leaves and broken eggshells; tissue paper in various colours; yellow raffia; paints; butterfly sponge shapes; red, black, yellow, brown and beige fabric; newspaper; tracing paper; cotton wool; black buttons; black pencils; simulated fur and feathers; silk poppies; ears of corn; clean eggshells; PVA glue; spreaders; paintbrushes; scissors; stapler; *Tattybogle* by Sandra Horn and Ken Brown (Andersen Press).

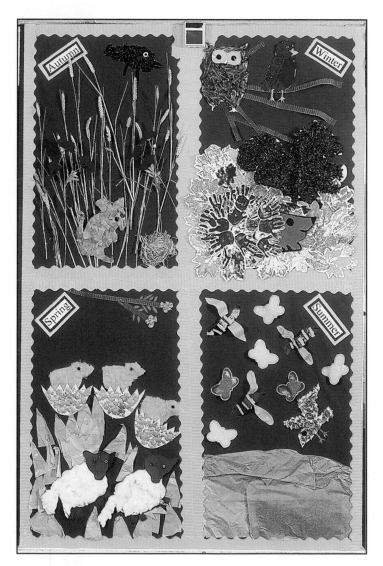

What to do

Cover a display board with backing paper. Make a frame and divide the board into four using a card border. Double mount labels with the names of the seasons on coloured paper and staple one to each section.

Gather the children together and read them the story of *Tattybogle*. Look at the pictures in the book and notice the animals and plants that Tattybogle sees through the seasons. Tell the children that they are going to make a display showing the animals that are seen at different times of the year.

Organize the children into groups to make the animals for each section.

● **Autumn:** stick squares of simulated fur or fabric to a mouse outline and staple this among real corn and silk poppies. Curl yellow raffia to make a nest shape. Make a blackbird by covering a template cut from black sugar paper with black tissue paper.

● **Winter:** print brown handprints, and leaf prints in autumn colours. Ask one child to paint the head and front legs of the hedgehog template. Staple the leaf prints across the bottom of the display. Cut out the handprints and glue onto the hedgehog to make spines. Paint on the eye, nose, mouth and feet of the hedgehog and staple him among the leaf prints. Make a squirrel from brown tissue and staple into position. Paint corrugated card brown to make branches and staple onto the backing paper. Make an owl by gluing layers of simulated feathers to a template cut from brown sugar paper. Add eyes made from small black sugar paper circles glued to larger yellow circles. Make the robin by gluing brown and red fabric squares onto a template. Staple the owl and the robin among the tree branches.

● **Spring:** ask a few children to cut green tissue paper triangles and glue them to the background for grass. Make a branch from painted corrugated card and glue on green leaves and blossom. Make chicks by gluing yellow fabric squares to templates and staple them across the middle of the display. Glue clean, broken eggshell to broken shell templates and staple underneath the chicks. Let the children paint black and white lambs, then add cotton wool to

Using the display
Personal, social and emotional development
● Make a list of rules to follow when observing animals in their natural environment.

Language and literacy
● Read stories and rhymes about animals such as *Frog in Winter* by Max Velthuijs (Andersen Press) or *What Fun to be a Hippo* with poems chosen by Wendy Cooling (Franklin Watts).

Mathematical development
● Compare the numbers of animals in the display. Are there more bees than lambs? How many mice are there?
● Count the legs on the animals. How many legs on one, two, three lambs?

Knowledge and understanding of the world
● Sort the animals into sets according to whether or not they can fly.
● Make a survey of the animals that can be seen around your setting. Sort them into minibeasts, birds and mammals.
● Collect pictures of different species of animals. Sort them according to whether or not they are found in this country.

Creative development
● Move like the different animals in the display. Use the music from *Carnival of the Animals* by Saint-Saëns to make up a simple routine. Add percussion accompaniments to enhance your performance!

give a textured effect to the fleeces. Add black buttons for eyes.
● **Summer:** make sea and sand from blue and yellow tissue paper. Invite the children to sponge-print butterfly shapes before cutting them out and sticking them into place. Stick scrunched-up newspaper to a seagull template. When dry, paint grey and then add a felt or button eye. Make bees with yellow and black fabric stripes glued to yellow sugar paper. Add tracing paper wings with veins drawn on using black pencils.

Talk about
● Discuss the animals in the picture. Can the children remember their names?
● Talk about the animals that can be seen all year round and those that are only seen at certain times during the year. Make picture lists of the outcome of your discussion.
● Talk about the animals in your display that hibernate. Explain that some animals sleep during the cold winter months and only wake up when the weather begins to get warmer.

Home links
● Ask parents and carers to help with the cutting out activities for the display.
● If you make this display in the spring, invite parents and carers to accompany you on a visit to a local farm to show the children the new animal life.

Interactive display

THEMES ON DISPLAY
for early years

Evergreen plants

Learning objective: to learn that some kinds of plants look the same all the year round.

What you need
Green backing paper; coloured lettering; green foil paper; green sugar paper; corrugated card; white paper; brown chalk; green paint; holly and ivy; thick green wool; twigs; PVA glue; spreaders; stapler; books about trees.

What to do
Cover a display board with green backing paper. Add the label 'Evergreen' made from coloured lettering.

Gather the children together and show them the holly and ivy. Explain to the children that these plants stay green all through the year, and so are called evergreens. Tell them that these plants are sometimes used as decoration at Christmas time. What other evergreens do we see at Christmas? If necessary, tell the children that some people decorate real Christmas trees, and these are also evergreens. Look at the books about trees and identify some evergreens. Explain that you would like the children to help you to make a display of evergreen plants.

Cut ivy leaf shapes from green sugar paper. Let the children stick on squares of green foil to make shiny ivy leaves. Staple these around the edge of the display to make a frame. Make stems to link the leaves by wrapping thick green wool around twigs and stapling them to the display.

Organize the children into two groups. Ask one group to make handprints using green paint. When dry, cut out the prints and glue in layers, like a tree, starting from the bottom. Colour a rectangle of paper with brown chalk and staple this into position for a trunk.

Using the display
Language and literacy
● Share story-books about trees such as *The Fir Tree* by Hans Christian Andersen and Bernadette Watts (North-South Books).
● Make up a group poem about a Christmas tree using words such as sharp, shiny, spiky, prickly and so on.

Mathematical development
● Collect some evergreen leaves and talk about the shapes. How many points are there on the holly leaves? What shapes are the fir tree needles?
● Sort evergreen leaves into sets of shiny/not shiny; prickly/not prickly and leaves/needles.

Knowledge and understanding of the world
● Develop computer skills by inviting the children to create labels for the different parts of the trees including roots, trunk, branches, twigs and leaves/needles.
● Take a walk in your local park to look for evergreen trees and plants.

Creative development
● Make evergreen trees using various techniques. Stick scraps of fabric to tree outlines, glue on real leaves or print using sponge or potato shapes.
● Design some Christmas wrapping paper using Christmas tree, ivy and holly shapes.

Make a fir tree by gluing triangles cut from green painted corrugated card to green sugar paper tree shapes. Colour or paint a brown trunk. Staple both trees to the display. Staple real holly around and among the trees and add labels.

At Christmas, place a decorated tree and wrapped presents in front of the evergreen display.

Talk about
● Talk about ivy and the holly berries. Reinforce the dangers of poisonous berries and plants. Tell the children that they must never eat berries or leaves.
● Look at the Christmas tree and compare it to the trees in the earlier display. How are the leaves different? Tell the children that this type of leaves are called needles.

Home links
● Ask parents and carers to reinforce the dangers of poisonous berries and other poisonous plants at home.
● Ask one or two adults to help the children to make the Christmas tree and ivy leaves.

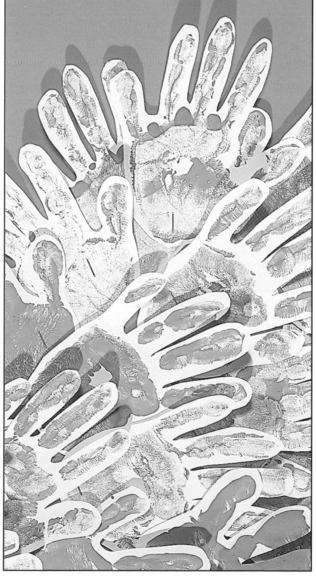

Interactive display

Weather forecast

Learning objective: to learn about the weather in summer and winter.

What you need
Neutral and pale blue backing paper; white card; blue card border; white paper; newspaper; grey and white paint; pale yellow paper; yellow tissue paper; scissors; PVA glue and spreaders; stapler, books about weather such as *Weather* by Sally Hewitt in the *It's Science!* series (Franklin Watts).

What to do
Cover the top half of a display board with neutral and the bottom half with pale blue backing paper. Fix a blue border around the edge. Staple labels for winter and summer to the top and bottom half of the display respectively.

Gather the children around the board and talk about today's weather. Is it sunny or cloudy? Cold or warm? Wet or dry? Explain that the weather is usually very different in winter and summer. Tell the children that it is usually much colder and rainier in winter and the sky is usually much bluer in summer. Let the children watch as you paint white strips across the blue section of the display to represent clouds. Tell the children that they are going to make the dark winter clouds for the top part of the display.

Encourage the children to glue scrunched-up newspaper to cloud shapes and then paint the finished collage grey. When dry, staple to the board. Next, ask the children to make two suns – one for winter and one for summer. Ask a small group to cut a semicircle and thin strips from pale yellow paper. Glue these to the top of

Using the display
Language and literacy
● Introduce the children to language that describes the weather such as rainy, wet, snowy, sunny, hot, warm, foggy, windy. Make up a group poem.
● Learn rhymes and poems about the weather such as 'Doctor Foster Went to Gloucester' and 'The North Wind Doth Blow' from *Sing Hey Diddle Diddle* (A & C Black).

Mathematical development
● Record the types of weather during each week. After a few weeks, count and compare the number of wet/dry/windy/foggy days.
● Learn the order of the days of the week, using appropriate language. Which day comes first? Which is the fourth day? Which day comes before Tuesday? After Sunday?

Knowledge and understanding of the world
● Put one large thermometer inside and one outside your setting and let the children compare them. Explain that the liquid in the thermometers goes up when it gets warmer and goes down when it gets colder.
● Use a drawing program on the computer to draw weather symbols.

Creative development
● Experiment with different percussion instruments to make weather sounds. Try to make quiet sounds to represent rain showers, and big loud crashes to represent thunder. Make up an accompaniment to the 'Seasons' poem on page 73.
● Create a dance about the different kinds of weather using appropriate music or percussion instruments.

the display. Make the summer sun trom a large circle and six triangles of yellow paper covered in bright yellow tissue paper. When dry, staple to the bottom half of the display and arrange the triangles around the circumference.

Arrange books about the weather in front of the display.

Talk about
● Talk about the names of different weather conditions such as mist, sleet, fog, drizzle and so on. Make a weatherboard to record the weather using labels of these words and more familiar weather words.
● Discuss some of the special clothes that we wear in certain kinds of weather.

Home links
● Ask parents and carers to discuss the day's weather with the children each morning, and to talk about the sorts of clothes that they should wear. This will give the children the confidence to join in with the discussions about the weather when they arrive at your group.

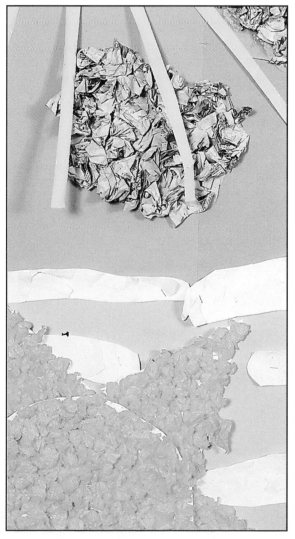

THEMES ON DISPLAY
for early years

Which season?

Learning objective: to learn that some things are used only in summer, spring, autumn or winter.

What you need
Sugar paper in various colours; coloured card; a collection of clothes and objects to represent each of the four seasons such as scarf, gloves, wellingtons, sun-hat, flip-flops, pictures of spring flowers, sun cream, conkers, hot-water bottle.

What to do
Cover a display surface using four different colours of paper to make four sections. Label each section with the appropriate season.

Show the children your collection of clothes and objects. Starting with the season that you are in, select one object and talk to the children about what it is. Can they tell you which season it belongs to? Place the object in the correct section telling the children the name of the season to reinforce learning. Repeat this until all of the objects have been placed in the appropriate sections.

Talk about
● Talk about the names of the four seasons. Remind the children of the name of the present season.

● Discuss the things that are in the current season's section. Are any of the objects used in the other seasons?

Home links
● Ask parents to contribute to the display by sending in relevant and unwanted items.
● Ask one or two parents and carers to come into the setting to help sort the objects with the children. Can any of the objects be used for more than one season? Put these together in a space by themselves.

Further display table ideas
● Make a collection of items for each season. For example, in autumn, make a display of fruits and nuts; in winter collect snow-scene toys; in spring grow some bulbs and display some spring flowers; in summer make a summer holiday collection.
● Make collections of colours associated with each season. For example red, orange, brown and yellow for autumn; white, black and silver for winter; yellow, orange and pink for spring; gold, blue and green for summer.
● Display animal models, postcards and pictures showing the animals seen during each of the seasons.
● Make a display of books, pictures and plants that remain green (evergreen) throughout the year.

Spring

Blossom trees

Learning objective: to learn that some trees are in blossom in springtime.

What you need
Pale blue backing paper; green paper; brown, white and red paint; brown sugar paper; newspaper; toothbrushes; paintbrushes; green and brown wax crayons; pink or white fabric; picture of a tree in blossom; several brown handprints; scissors; stapler.

What to do
Cover a display board with pale blue backing paper and green paper across the bottom to represent grass.

If possible, take the children outside and show them a tree that is in blossom. Alternatively, look at a picture. Point out the different parts of the tree including the trunk, branches, twigs, leaf buds and flowers. Talk about the colours and shapes of the leaf buds and flowers. Back inside, talk about the trees. Explain that some trees come into blossom in spring, just before they grow their leaves. Invite the children to help you to make a colourful blossom tree display.

Show the children how to use outstretched hands to make handprint trees on brown paper. Using a handprint that you made earlier, show them how to make a small blossom tree by dipping a finger into white paint and dabbing around the ends of the 'branches'. Demonstrate how to mix red and white paint to make pink, and then use the same technique to add pink blossom to another handprint tree. Organize the children into groups to make trees for the border.

Finally, make a large tree for the centre. Use toothbrushes to stroke brown paint onto brown paper strips for the trunk and branches. When dry, staple these to the display board, stuffing newspaper behind the trunk to create a three-dimensional effect. Invite a group of children to use wax crayons to add leaf buds. Ask the children whether they want pink or white blossom and add this to the large tree with small flower shapes cut from pink or white fabric.

Talk about
● Discuss the colours and shapes of the different parts of the tree.
● Talk about other plants that are in bloom at this time of year. Discuss snowdrops, daffodils and crocuses, and look at examples outside if possible.

Home links
● Ask parents and carers to look for and point out blossom trees on their journey to your setting.
● Invite extra adults into your setting to support the handprinting activity.

The season of spring is full of colour and vibrancy, and this chapter contains plenty of ideas to celebrate it to the full, from a display which focuses on wet and windy weather, to a beautiful blossom tree.

Spring

Easter

Learning objective: to find out about the festival of Easter.

What you need
Coloured backing paper; boxed Easter egg; selection of foils and shiny papers; large egg shape cut from cardboard; crêpe paper in various colours; cardboard egg box lids; tissue paper in various colours; pearlescent paint; paintbrushes; strips of card; felt-tipped pens; glitter pens; doilies; ribbon; brightly-coloured tissue paper; copies of the photocopiable sheet on page 74; PVA glue; spreaders; scissors; stapler.

What to do
Cover a display board with backing paper and add a title.

Talk to the children about Easter. Tell them that Easter is a Christian festival which celebrates Jesus' return to life. Because of this, Easter is associated with symbols of new life, and this is why people give eggs at this time. What else do we see at Easter? Talk about Easter bonnets, bunnies, hot cross buns, chicks and so on. Tell the children that you would like them to help you to make a display which celebrates Easter.

Show the children your boxed Easter egg and then invite them to decorate the large cardboard Easter egg shape by gluing on coloured and shiny paper. When it is covered, make a large bow from crêpe paper and fix it around the centre of the egg. Staple the egg to the display board.

Give each child a copy of the photocopiable sheet. Invite them to use felt-tipped pens and glitter pens to trace over the patterns to make colourful egg pictures. Use the finished pictures to make a border.

Make Easter baskets with the children. Paint egg box lids with pearlescent paint and add colourful handles made from strips of card covered with coloured and shiny paper. Fill the baskets with the children's choice of coloured tissue paper.

Make Easter bonnets from shiny paper and doilies. Add ribbons and tissue paper flowers, then attach them to the display board.

Cover the surface in front of the display with fabric or drapes and display your Easter baskets ready for the Easter bunny to visit!

Talk about
● Talk about the papers in your collection. Make a collection of any colours with which the children are not familiar. Talk about the

Using the display
Personal, social and emotional development
● Read the Easter story as told in the Bible (Matthew Chapters 26, 27 and 28). Explain that this story is believed by Christians. Be sensitive to the beliefs of children from different faiths in your setting.
● Encourage the children to work together to make the large egg. Remind them to share the glitter pens and to take turns to stick pieces of paper to the outline.

Language and literacy
● Look around your setting for objects that begin with the sound 'e'. Make a collection and draw pictures.
● Read stories about Easter such as *The Easter Story* by Heather Amery and Norman Young (Usborne).

Mathematical development
● Make a collection of objects with curved faces and sides including circles, cones, spheres and ovoids.

Knowledge and understanding of the world
● Organize an Easter egg hunt around your setting. Plot the positions of the hidden eggs on a large wall-mounted map before letting the children begin their hunt.

Physical development
● Mould Plasticine or play dough into egg shapes. Decorate them by stamping on patterns with modelling tools, then place them in decorated egg cups.

Creative development
● Make hot cross buns. Remind the children of the significance of the cross as they make their buns.
● Make Easter cards by folding A4 card so that the front opens up as two flaps (see diagram above). Let the children collage, draw or paint a complete egg on the front, and stick a yellow chick inside. Open up the front flaps to reveal the Easter chick!
● Sing 'My Easter Bonnet' from *Harlequin* (A & C Black).

appearance and textures of the different types of papers.
● Discuss the shape of an egg. Does it have any straight edges or corners? Is it curved?

Home links
● Ask additional adults to support the Easter egg hunt (see 'Knowledge and understanding of the world' left). Brief adults beforehand so that they can help the children to consider the positions of the hidden eggs from the map before they begin their hunt.
● Invite parents and carers to play colour- and shape-matching games with the children.

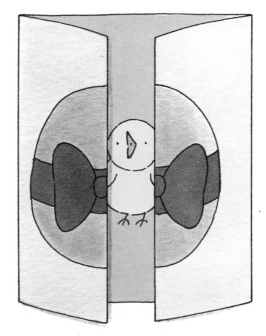

Spring

Beautiful bulbs

Learning objective: to learn that some flowers grow from bulbs.

What you need
Blue backing paper; cardboard boxes; sugar and poster paper in various colours; daffodils, tulips, crocuses and hyacinths; a bowl of indoor bulbs which have started to grow; brown fabric; large bowl template; egg boxes; yellow and orange paint; tissue paper in various colours; paintbrushes; yellow, purple and white pastels; blue buttons; green garden canes; sequins; PVA glue; spreaders; stapler; scissors; labels.

What to do
Cover a display board with pale blue paper. Cover the cardboard boxes with coloured paper.

Show the children the bowl of indoor bulbs. Carefully remove one entire bulb and flower from the container and examine it, noticing the roots at one end and the shoot at the other. Talk about how these bulbs stay in the soil over winter, and only begin to grow when the weather gets warmer in the spring. Has anyone noticed any green shoots in their garden or on their journey to your setting?

Explain to the children that many plants grow from bulbs, showing examples if possible. Tell them that some flowers also grow from seeds.

Look at all the spring flowers and explain that these were all grown from bulbs. Tell the children that you are going to make a display of spring flowers which grow from bulbs.

Organize a group of children to make the bowl. Show them how to apply PVA glue to stick coloured paper squares to the bowl template. Add brown fabric squares to represent soil, then staple the finished bowl to the board.

Invite other children to make various flowers using a variety of techniques:
- daffodils – cut six petal shapes from yellow poster paper and arrange them in a circle. Glue a painted egg box section in the centre. Alternatively, roll yellow or orange tissue paper into a cylinder shape and fix to the centre of the daffodil petals. Staple green garden canes to each side of the bowl and glue a daffodil flower at the top of each cane.
- tulips – cut petals from red, yellow and orange poster paper and arrange to make flower heads. Add stems and leaves made from tissue paper.
- crocuses – use purple, yellow and white pastel crayons to draw crocuses on large sheets of pale green sugar paper.

Using the display

Personal, social and emotional development

● Remind the children that they should never pick flowers that grow in the wild such as bluebells, daffodils and cowslips (which are protected), or in people's gardens.
● What do the bulbs need in order to grow? Talk about water, warmth and light. What would happen if the bulbs were not watered?

Language and literacy

● Organize the role-play area into a garden centre. Sell a wide selection of gardening equipment as well as empty seed packets, bulbs of different shapes and sizes, artificial flowers and gardening books.

Knowledge and understanding of the world

● Let the children close their eyes and smell the flowers. Which smell the strongest – hyacinths or daffodils?
● Visit a local garden centre to see the range of spring bulbs and flowers.

Creative development

● Use a variety of techniques to create flower pictures. Try printing with potatoes, using fabric paints or making finger-print pictures.
● Use flower designs to make wrapping paper for Easter presents.

● hyacinths – glue circles of white, pink and blue tissue paper either side of green paper stems.
● bluebells – decorate vases with flowers and sequins and fill them with bluebells made from blue tissue paper shapes and green garden canes.

Add labels of the colours and names of the flowers and a border made from different coloured paper. Arrange the spring flowers and bulbs on the covered boxes in front of the display.

Talk about

● Discuss the colours of spring flowers.
● Compare the colour, size and shape of the petals and leaves between two of the types of flower.
● Go on a short walk around the setting to notice and recognize the flowers in the surrounding environment.

Home links

● Send home a letter to parents and carers to explain the purpose of the display. Ask them to point out spring flowers to the children when they are out and about.
● Make a lucky dip bag of crocus and daffodil bulbs. Let each child pick two or three bulbs to take home and grow. They will love the anticipation of waiting for their flowers to grow before they can identify them!
● Ask for extra adults to accompany you on a short walk around your setting or local area to look at spring flowers.

March winds and April showers

Learning objective: to find out about the wet and windy weather in March and April.

What you need

Pale blue backing paper; black paper; brown fabric; newspaper; blue and silver foil; thin thread; paints; paper; wool; paintbrushes; scissors; fabric offcuts in various colours; cloud and umbrella templates; colourful braids, buttons, ribbons and papers; white paper banner; felt-tipped pens; collection of children's clothing for windy and wet days; old umbrella and rainhat; PVA glue and spreaders; stapler; lettering.

What to do

Cover a display board with pale blue backing paper and divide with a strip of black paper. To the left-hand side, staple brown fabric, gathered and stretched to look like a tree being blown by the wind. Stuff newspaper behind the tree to give a three-dimensional effect.

Talk to the children about the weather in March and April. Explain that as we move from winter to summer, the weather is often changeable, and can be dry and calm one minute, but rainy and windy the next. Explain that this is why March is often windy and April is often rainy. The short spells of rain that we frequently get at this time of year are called showers.

Invite the children to paint a picture of a person on a windy day. What sort of clothes might they wear? Would their hair look neat and tidy or windswept? Ask the children to make clouds, umbrellas and raindrops. Glue scrunched-up newspaper to cloud shapes and, when dry, paint them white. Cut out one of the children's paintings and staple the person into position. Add an old umbrella turned inside out by the wind and a hat being blown away. Add some windswept wool hair to the person!

Cut raindrops from silver and blue foil, and let the children add these to the display board. Cut out three umbrella shapes and encourage the children to add patterns using coloured braids, buttons, ribbons and fabric or paper offcuts. Staple among the raindrops.

Add lettering to make the titles 'March winds' and 'April showers' on the appropriate sections. Across the bottom of the board, add a banner with the words 'bring forth

Using the display

Personal, social and emotional development

● Read 'The Sun and the Wind' from *Aesop's Fables* retold by Anne Gatti (Pavilion Books). Talk about the morals in the story.

Language and literacy

● Read the poem 'Wind' by Shirley Hughes in *Out and About Through the Year* (Walker Books). Explore rainy and windy words. Make a display by attaching windy words to a large grey cloud shape, and suspending rainy words on shiny raindrops underneath the cloud.

Mathematical development

● During March and April, keep a tally of the number of windy and rainy days. Were there more rainy days or dry days? Show the information as tallies, pictograms or graphs.

Knowledge and understanding of the world

● Input the data from your tally chart into a data-handling program on the computer. Show the information as pictorial charts and simple graphs.
● Talk about things that we do in windy and rainy weather. Discuss kites, yachts and balloons, which are moved by the force of the wind.
● Take the children out on a windy day. Let them each hold a large sheet of paper or a long ribbon to experience the force of the wind.

Physical development

● Make up mimes based on the weather. Pretend to jump and splash in puddles, huddle up warm against the wind, fly a kite or put up an umbrella.

Creative development

● Make some lively windy and rainy day pictures by blowing paint through a straw or flicking it from old toothbrushes.
● Learn the song 'In All Kinds of Weather' from *Tinderbox* (A & C Black). Use percussion instruments to add simple accompaniments. Create a windy weather dance and perform it to parents and carers.

May flowers', decorated with the children's pictures. Suspend foil raindrops in front of the 'April showers' section. Add items of children's clothing that are worn on windy and rainy days, labelled appropriately.

Talk about

● Say the rhyme 'March winds and April showers, bring forth May flowers'. Make up some other verses with the children to extend the rhyme.

Home links

● Ask parents and carers to help groups of children to make the raindrops and attach them to the display.
● Invite parents to contribute wet and windy weather clothing and accessories to add to the display.

THEMES ON DISPLAY
for early years

New life

Learning objective: to learn about the new life that begins in springtime.

What you need
Green backing paper and fabric; paints; felt-tipped pens; paintbrushes; white and yellow paper; white, black, green and yellow fabric; cotton wool; yellow pipe-cleaners; feathers; black buttons and sequins; straw; animal toys; bubble wrap; books and pictures of baby animals; animal sponges; Blu-Tack; PVA glue; spreaders; scissors; stapler.

What to do
Cover a display board with green backing paper and invite some children to paint spring flowers to stick onto the background. Add a blossom tree and the title 'New Life'.

Gather the children together. Share the books and pictures of baby animals. Invite the children to share their experiences of seeing or even touching baby animals. Some may have visited a farm where they were allowed to stroke the animals. Tell the children that some animals, such as foals and lambs can be born as early as January. Invite the children to help you to make a display showing some of the animals that we see in spring.

Organize the children into groups to make different animals. To make a chick, draw two circles, one larger than the other, for the head and body. Cut the circles out and paint, colour or cover with fabric. Add yellow pipe-cleaner legs, paper triangles for the beak and a black sequin for the eye. Make a mother hen and then attach the hen and chicks to the board in a group. Make goslings and ducklings in the same way, using appropriate templates and colours and making round-edged beaks and webbed feet.

Make a nest from straw. Cut circles from black paper and add black sequins for eyes. Make an open beak from yellow paper triangles. Staple the nest into the crook of a branch of the blossom tree and add the baby birds. Add an adult bird nearby and label appropriately.

Make a pond from pale green paper and invite the children to use black felt-tipped pens to draw tadpoles in the water. Add bubble wrap with black dots added for frog's spawn. Add an adult frog.

Use fabric, paint and cotton wool to make pictures of sheep, lambs, horses, foals, cows and calves and add these to the display. Use Blu-Tack to add a border of postcards or pictures. Alternatively, sponge-print animals for a border.

Place the green fabric in front of the display and invite the children to arrange the animals from the farm or those collected from home. Make free-standing labels and display the books among them.

Using the display

Personal, social and emotional development

● Talk about the need to look after young animals and plant life. Reinforce the message that nesting birds should never be disturbed. Tell the children that if they touch or visit a nest before the baby birds have left, the adult birds will abandon their young and they will die. It is also an offence to remove frog's spawn from its natural habitat.

● Talk about caring for the environment so that animals' habitats are not destroyed by our careless actions.

Language and literacy

● Talk about the names of young animals including chicks, lambs, piglets, calves, foals, ducklings, goslings and kids.

● Draw or stick pictures of the animals on the appropriate labels. Each day, place the labels in a box and ask the children to match the correct label to each animal on the display.

Mathematical development

● Count the numbers of each animal in the display.

● Sort the animals into sets according to the number of legs.

● Learn a selection of animal number rhymes such as 'Five Little Speckled Frogs' from *Apusskidu* (A & C Black) or 'One, Two, Three, Four, Five' and 'Five Brown Eggs' both from *This Little Puffin...* compiled by Elizabeth Matterson (Puffin).

Knowledge and understanding of the world

● Sort the animals into sets according to the ways in which they move.

● Match the baby animals to their adult partner.

● Use a CD-ROM to find information about some of the animals found in the display.

Physical development

● Develop a movement sequence based on the way that the different animals move.

Creative development

● Sing songs about animals such as 'Old MacDonald Had a Farm' (Traditional) and 'Chicks Grow into Chickens' from *Birds and Beasts* (A & C Black). Make appropriate actions to accompany the songs.

Talk about

● Discuss the names of the different animals in the display. Can the children tell you the adult name for each baby animal?

● Talk about the birds' feet. Why do ducks and geese have webbed feet?

● Talk about what each of the animals can do. Which animals can fly, swim and gallop, for example?

Home links

● Ask additional adults to accompany the group on a visit to a farm to see some baby animals.

● Ask parents and carers to send in items for the display including animal models, ornaments and toys, books, pictures and postcards.

● Following your setting's policy, invite an adult to come into the setting to talk about, and maybe bring in, a baby animal to show the children.

Spring cleaning

Learning objective: to understand that people 'spring clean'.

What you need

Pale blue and green backing paper; cardboard boxes; yellow fabric; felt-tipped pens; green and white tissue paper; white chalk; cardboard; paints; paintbrushes; sugar paper in various colours; gummed paper; blue Cellophane; scissors; PVA glue and spreaders; cleaning materials including dusters, carpet sweeper, dustpan and brush, broom, mop, bucket, feather dusters, sponges and non-toxic cleaning substances such as polish and soap; child's bucket; stapler.

What to do

Cover a display board with pale blue and green backing paper to represent the sky and the grass. Arrange the cardboard boxes across the display surface and cover them with yellow fabric. Add the title 'Spring cleaning'. Lightly spread white chalk across the top of the paper to make wispy clouds.

Gather the children together and show them the collection of cleaning materials. Talk about the purpose of each one and how it is used. As you talk about the items add them to the display surface. Talk about spring cleaning. Explain that when the weather gets warmer, people often decide to tidy and clean everything around them, and this is called spring cleaning. Tell the children that you are going to make a picture together to show how people spring clean their homes and gardens.

Organize a group of children to make a house by cutting and sticking red sugar paper rectangles onto a large square shape. Let another group stick black sugar paper rectangles to a trapezium shape to make roof tiles. Cut out rectangles for windows and stick blue Cellophane to the back. Make a door from gummed paper. Fix the house and roof to the display board.

Ask a group of children to make gummed paper flowers and tissue paper grass, and glue them to the board.

Ask two pairs of children to paint a front and back view of two people and when dry, cut them out. Ask another child to paint a picture of a lawn mower. Cut out the rungs of a ladder from appropriately coloured sugar paper and staple into position beneath one upstairs window. Staple the back view of the person to the ladder and attach a sponge to their hand. Hang a child's bucket from the top rung of the ladder. Add the lawn mower and the remaining person.

Finally, add sentences describing the cleaning activities taking place in the display such as, 'Dad is cleaning the windows' and 'Mum is cutting the grass'. Invite the children to add

more pictures and sentences to the display at a later date.

Talk about
● Discuss the cleaning activities that the children do at home. Do they help to tidy their room? What other things do their parents or carers clean, such as windows, the floor and so on? What do they use to clean these things?
● Talk about cleaning and tidying tools which use electricity such as lawn mowers and vacuum cleaners. Reinforce the dangers of electricity, reminding the children that they must not touch wires and sockets.

Home links
● Ask parents and carers to loan or contribute interesting items to the display such as brightly-coloured feather dusters or old-fashioned cleaning items.
● Invite one or two adults to make some simple shape-matching games for the children to play at your setting. Ask them to make baseboards and cards using brightly-coloured circles, rectangles, triangles, squares and ovals.

Using the display
Personal, social and emotional development
● Talk about the dangers of cleaning substances and materials. Emphasize that the children should never touch them unless an adult is with them.
● Discuss how the children can help at home by putting toys away or weeding the garden.

Language and literacy
● Make a book of words and pictures about cleaning and tidying activities.
● Initiate some role-play as the children spring clean the home corner.

Mathematical development
● Let the children make pictures and patterns using lots of different gummed paper shapes.

Knowledge and understanding of the world
● Look at pictures and books of things in and around the home and talk about how they would be cleaned. Sort them into sets according to whether they are washed, polished or tidied away.
● Look at pictures or real examples of things that people used a long time ago to spring clean their homes such as a flat iron, a washboard and a washing dolly. Can the children suggest how they were used?

Creative development
● Make up a song with the children about cleaning, to the tune of 'Here We Go Round the Mulberry Bush' (Traditional). Develop some actions to accompany the song.

Table-top display

THEMES ON DISPLAY
for early years

Spring things!

Learning objective: to explore things that are seen in spring.

What you need
Green fabric; cardboard boxes; coloured paper; a box containing a collection of items found in springtime including books, ornaments, items with spring designs; labels.

What to do
Cover a display surface with green fabric. Cover the cardboard boxes with coloured paper and arrange them to create different levels of interest. Talk to the children about springtime and remind them of all the things that you have talked about. Explain that you are going to make a display of lots of things that remind us of spring.

Invite a child to select an item from the box and hold it up for the others to see. Talk about the item and decide together where to put it on the display. Write a label and place it by the item. Continue until all the items in your collection have been placed onto the display table.

Invite the children to add to the display over the next few days. Every day, gather together in front of the display and add the additional items.

Talk about
● Talk about the colours in the display. Can the children name them?
● Discuss any unusual items that you have in your collection, such as a vase in the shape of a tulip or a scarf decorated with spring flowers.
● Talk about the initial sounds on the labels. Do these help to match the item to its label?

Home links
● Invite parents and carers to contribute to the display with unusual items. Provide ideas as to where they may find items, such as in charity shops or at car boot sales.
● Write to supermarkets and other outlets asking them for discarded items from their spring displays.

Further display table ideas
● Make a display using objects in bright spring colours such as yellow, orange and pink. Intersperse your collection with daffodils, tulips, crocuses and blossoms.
● Make a collection of items and pictures of things used to spring clean bedrooms.
● Display a collection of umbrellas with different patterns and pictures with items of clothing that would be worn in wet weather.

Summer

Summer sun

Learning objective: to find out that the sun gives us light and heat.

What you need
Pale blue backing paper; yellow card; gold foil; gold and yellow sugar paper, tissue paper; crêpe paper; gold and yellow fabric; PVA glue; spreaders; scissors; yellow paint; paintbrushes; stapler.

What to do
Cover a small display board with pale blue backing paper.

Cut a large yellow circle measuring approximately 50cm in diameter from yellow sugar paper. Cut out squares of yellow fabric, crêpe paper, sugar paper and tissue paper.

Show the children how to use small amounts of the PVA glue on their spreader to stick the various yellow squares all over the circle. Fill in the spaces with yellow paint. Staple the circle to the centre of the display board.

Cut long, thin triangles from yellow card to go all the way around the edge of the circle. Glue gold foil and crêpe paper squares all over the triangles.

When dry, staple these around the edge of the sun so that they extend over the edges of the board. Add a title if you wish.

Talk about
● Talk about the heat of the sun on a hot day. Have any of the children been on holiday to a hot country? Can they tell the other children about it?
● Talk about sunrise and sunset. Explain that when the sun rises in the morning, it starts to get light and when it goes down at night, it starts to get dark.
● Explain to the children that they should never look directly at the sun as it can damage their eyes.

Home links
● Ask parents and carers to reinforce the message that it is very dangerous to look directly at the sun as it can seriously damage the eyesight.
● Invite adults to collect or come into the setting to cut out pictures of the sun to use for additional summer activities.

The long sunny days of summer are the inspiration for this collection of sun and fun-filled displays, which also bring home the important message of sun safety.

Interactive display

What shall we wear?

Learning objective: to understand that we wear lighter and thinner clothes in summer.

What you need
Blue backing paper; green tissue paper; silver and gold foil; red poster paper; cardboard tubes; red, yellow, green and black paint; white paper; string; corrugated card; PVA glue; scissors; stapler; felt-tipped pens.

What to do
Begin by talking about the season of summer with the children. What do they like about summer? Talk about the things that people do on warm summer days and the type of clothes that they might wear. What would the children wear to play in the park on a summer's day? What about on a trip to the seaside? Tell the children that you would like their help to make a sunny display showing the clothes that people wear in summer.

Cover a display board with blue backing paper. Cut tall isosceles triangles from white paper and ask the children to paint them in different shades of green. When dry, coat them with PVA glue. Staple them into place at the bottom of the board to create a variety of textured grass.

Attach a slide made from a large sheet of silver foil edged with red poster paper. Add steps cut from the red poster paper.

Ask a child to make a seat for a swing by painting a rectangular piece of corrugated card black. Ask another group to paint the cardboard tubes red.

When dry, staple the tubes in the centre of the board to make the frame of the swing. Plait several lengths of string, then attach these to the top of the swing and staple the seat in place.

Give each child a sheet of paper and a selection of felt-tipped pens, and ask them to draw a picture of themselves wearing summer clothes, using the whole piece of paper. Cut the pictures out and mount them onto paper of a contrasting colour. Cut around the outlines and staple them to the display on the grass, swing and slide.

Invite a small group of children to paint a large yellow circle to make the centre of the sun. Glue gold foil triangles to the back of the circle to make the sun's rays, then staple into position at the top of the display. Add a title if you wish.

Talk about
● Talk to the children about the clothes that they wear in summer. Are the clothes thick or thin? Can the children name any of the materials that the clothes are made from? Why do we wear thinner and lighter (less heavy) clothes in summer? How would we feel if we wore thick coats and jumpers when the weather was very hot?
● Compare a set of winter and summer clothes. Talk about the similarities and differences.

Using the display
Personal, social and emotional development
● Play some playground games such as 'In and Out the Dusty Bluebells' or 'Ring-o-Ring-o-Roses' in *This Little Puffin...* compiled by Elizabeth Matterson (Puffin).

Language and literacy
● Read *Mrs Mopple's Washing Line* by Anita Hewett and Robert Broomfield (Red Fox) substituting the items of clothing in the story with summer ones. Have a set of clothing to show to the children as you read the story.
● Name the items of clothing that the children wear in the summer.

Mathematical development
● Introduce or reinforce the name of the triangle and rectangle shape. Identify these shapes in the display.
● Play the shape matching game on the photocopiable sheet on page 75.

Knowledge and understanding of the world
● Reinforce the names of the different parts of the body, using the children's drawings for reference.
● Make a large, simple map of the route to the local playground and a plan of the layout of the equipment.

Creative development
● Role-play a trip to the seaside or the playground. Encourage the children to mop their brows and shield their eyes as they might if they were out in the sun!

● Discuss the different kinds of equipment in the local park or playground. Ask the children to name them. How do they play on each one?
● Reinforce the safety issues when playing on equipment in the local playground.

Home links
● Ask one or two parents or carers to accompany the children on an outing to the local park to see and play on the playground equipment.
● Invite a few adults to support the children in their drawings of themselves. Ask them to reinforce the names and positions of the different parts of the body, and the type of clothes that the children wear in the summertime.

Summer fête

Learning objective: to think about events that happen in the summer.

What you need
A table; green and grey backing paper; sugar paper in bright colours; paints; paintbrushes; collage materials; newspaper; paste; balloons; coloured foil; ribbon; PVA glue; white paper; cardboard tubes; red and yellow crêpe paper; apple shapes; red and green wax crayons; lollipop sticks; sticky tape; tall, empty tins; cotton wool; stapler; clear plastic box; pink powder paint; garden canes; Blu-Tack.

What to do
Talk about events that happen in the summer. Have the children ever been to a fair or a fête? Maybe you have held one at your setting. Encourage them to suggest things that they might see at a fête such as bouncy castles, hook-a-duck, candy-floss stalls, balloons and so on. Invite the children to help you make a colourful display of a summer fête.

Cover a display board with green and grey backing paper to represent the grass and playground. Make a bouncy castle with coloured paper coated with PVA glue to give a shiny effect. Ask the children to paint or collage pictures of people visiting the fête. When dry, mount them onto contrasting paper, cut them out, and staple them on and around the bouncy castle.

Blow up some balloons and invite the children to work together to paste on several layers of newspaper strips. When dry, cut the balloons in half. Add a layer of silver foil and decorate with different-coloured foils. Staple the balloons to the display and use ribbon to attach them to the figures.

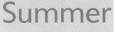
Using the display
Personal, social and emotional development
● Develop the children's ability to share and take turns by playing summer games.

Language and literacy
● Make posters and invitations advertising your fête.
● Read *Dogger* by Shirley Hughes (Red Fox). Talk about the different stalls and games at the fête.

Mathematical development
● Play 'Guess the number of sweets in a jar'. Vary the number of sweets according to the age and ability of your children.
● Use a tombola to develop the children's understanding of numbers of odd or even numbers. If the prizes are sweets for odd numbers and balloons for even numbers, what will they win if they pick the number 7? What about the number 4?

Knowledge and understanding of the world
● Make a treasure map to find some 'hidden treasure' in and around your setting.
● Each morning, hide some treasure in the sand tray and show where it is hidden on an accompanying plan. Challenge the children to try to locate the treasure by referring to the plan.

Physical development
● Set up some target games such as throwing a hoopla into numbered squares, throwing beanbags into hoops or buckets or rolling tennis balls to knock down skittles.

Cover a table with strips of red and yellow crêpe paper. Wind narrow strips of crêpe paper around two cardboard tubes and fix these to the front corners of the table. Cover a large sheet of white paper with red and yellow crêpe paper and fasten it to the wall, and to the cardboard tubes to make a canopy. Make toffee apples by colouring apple shapes in red and green wax crayon and attaching them to lollipop sticks with tape. Shake together some cotton wool and pink powder paint in the plastic box. Fix to garden canes to make candy floss. Stand the toffee apples and candy floss in tins covered with coloured foil.

Talk about
● Talk about the children's experiences of visits to fêtes or fairs. What stalls did they visit? Did they win anything?

Home links
● Organize a summer fête and invite parents and carers to help out.
● Ask parents and carers to contribute inexpensive prizes for a tombola.
● Hire a bouncy castle for the day. Follow the safety policy for your setting.
● Ask parents to come into your setting to play some summer fête games, such as guess the number of sweets in a jar, treasure trails or a children's tombola.

Fields of flowers

Learning objective: to learn about summer flowers.

What you need
Green backing paper; yellow, green and blue tissue paper; white, black and yellow paint; green and yellow paper; paintbrushes; scissors; PVA glue; spreader; gold foil; wheat; yellow wool; yellow Cellophane; card circles; cotton wool; stapler.

What to do
Begin by taking the children outside if possible to look at some summer flowers. Find and identify some daisies, clover, buttercups or dandelions. Notice the bright, sunny colours and let the children investigate the shape and size of the petals, leaves, stems and so on.

Back indoors, invite the children to use their observations to make a colourful display of summer flowers. Cover a display board with green backing paper and yellow and blue tissue paper to depict grass, wheat fields and sky. Staple ears of wheat to the yellow tissue paper.

Invite the children to cut out triangles from green tissue paper and glue these to the green backing paper to make textured grass.

Ask the children to print white handprints on green paper. When dry, cut them out and staple six in a circle to make daisies. Make the centres by sticking scraps of yellow paper and Cellophane to circles of green paper.

Make buttercups by cutting heart shapes from white paper and painting with thick yellow paint. When dry, cover with PVA glue to give a shiny effect. Staple five or six hearts in a circle and add centres made in the same way as the daisies.

To make clover, let the children dab cotton wool clusters with black paint. Attach to the display and paint on black stems. Make dandelions by gluing yellow wool to card circles. Again, paint on thin black stems after attaching the dandelions carefully to the display.

Finish the display with a sun made from a circle of yellow paper and rays of gold foil. Add a title if you wish.

SEASONS

Talk about
● Discuss the flowers that you saw around your setting. Tell the children that these flowers are 'wild' – they are not planted but they grow every year. Compare them to garden flowers, which are planted specifically to make gardens look pretty.
● Explain to the children that they should not pick wild flowers as some are protected.

Home links
● Ask parents and carers to send in photographs of flowers which grow in the summer.
● Send a letter home explaining what the children have been learning. Ask parents and carers to point out different summer flowers on their journey to and from your setting, paying particular attention to the wild flowers in your display.

Using the display
Language and literacy
● Learn the names of some summer flowers. Bring in examples and display them in clearly labelled vases.

Mathematical development
● Describe the shapes of the flowers, petals and leaves. Identify the curving parts of the petals and leaves, and the straight stems.
● Count the petals on the buttercups. Which has more petals – a buttercup or a daisy?
● Compare the sizes of the flowers. Which is the biggest? Which is the smallest? Compare other flowers, such as sunflowers and daisies.

Knowledge and understanding of the world
● Make a collection of pictures and photographs of summer flowers. Sort them into wild flowers and garden flowers. Explain the difference between the two sets.
● Sprinkle some wild flower seeds onto an area of garden by your setting and watch them grow.

Creative development
● Make observational paintings of the various summer flowers, inviting the children to carefully mix their own shades of paint.
● Learn the song 'English Country Garden' from *Harlequin* (A & C Black).

THEMES ON DISPLAY
for early years

Sunny days

Learning objective: to learn that there are more hours of daylight in summer than in winter.

What you need
A clock face; green backing paper; green and orange tissue paper; red and orange Cellophane; yellow and blue fabric; corrugated card; white and coloured A3 paper; white card; paint in various colours; string; paintbrushes; felt-tipped pens; PVA glue; spreaders; scissors.

What to do
Cover your display area with green backing paper and add some tissue paper grass. Attach a clock face with the hands set at five o'clock.

Gather the children together and initiate a discussion about summer days. What do the children do on summer afternoons and evenings? How is a summer evening different to a winter evening? Think of some games that people might play during the long summer evenings, such as skipping, football or tennis. Explain that you are going to make a display showing some of the things that the children might do on a summer's evening.

Provide paints, felt-tipped pens and paper and invite the children to paint or draw a picture of themselves dressed in summer clothes. When dry, cut out and mount them onto contrasting paper then cut around the outlines.

Make tennis rackets by gluing screwed-up orange tissue paper to a cut-out frame. Criss-cross lengths of

Using the display
Personal, social and emotional development
● Play games with bats and balls to encourage the children to share and co-operate.

Language and literacy
● Reinforce the names of different times of the day. Make a wall frieze of pictures showing activities that the children do at different times of the day and encourage the children to arrange them in order. Label the pictures with the children's sentences.

Mathematical development
● What shape are the cricket and tennis balls in the display? Find other examples of circles and spheres around your setting.

● Look at the clock with the children. Talk about the position of the hands. Can the children see that the hand pointing to the 12 is longer than the hand pointing to the 5? Explain that when the long hand is pointing to the 12 it always means o'clock. Use a play clock to show different times.

Physical development
● On a warm day, take the children outside and play games using lots of different equipment. How do they feel when they have been running around in the hot weather?

Creative development
● Make up a song to the tune of 'Here We Go Round the Mulberrry Bush' about the things that the children do on summer evenings.

string across the frame to make the strings. Glue yellow and blue fabric to a circle of card to make a tennis ball. Staple two of the children's pictures to the display, each holding a tennis racket, and with the ball between them.

Draw the outline of a cricket bat on white paper and invite one child to paint it. Make cricket stumps from strips of corrugated card painted brown, and staple to the display in the shape of a wicket before adding two cut-out children, each holding a cricket bat. Paint a circle of card to make a red ball and staple it between the two children.

Make a setting sun by sticking scraps of red and orange Cellophane to a large circle cut from white paper. Add a title if desired.

Talk about
● Talk about other activities that the children might do during the light summer evenings such as going swimming, playing in the park, playing with their pets and so on.
● Talk about summer sports that the children might see on television such as cricket, tennis, swimming and athletics.

Home links
● Find out whether any of your parents and carers participate in any summer sports. Invite them to talk to the children about their sport and the clothes that they wear.
● Ask parents and carers to help develop children's knowledge of time by drawing their attention to the clock when it reaches five o'clock. Invite them to make a note of what they were doing and then to share this with everybody the next day. Was it dark at five o'clock?

THEMES ON DISPLAY
for early years

Shady places

Learning objective: to learn that it is important to keep covered up in the hot sun.

What you need
Brown tissue paper; shades of green tissue paper; leaf shapes; green backing paper; corrugated card; orange and red Cellophane; PVA glue; spreaders; brown paint; paintbrushes; white paper; brown wax crayons; yellow and red fabric; cardboard tube; scissors; paper plates and cups; stapler; bread; toaster (or pre-toasted bread).

What to do
Use this display to reinforce the dangers of staying out for too long in the sun. Let the children watch as you make a piece of toast, or show them the toasted bread. Tell them that, just as the hot elements in the toaster burn the bread and turn it into toast, the sun can burn our skins. Can they suggest any ways of keeping safe in the sun? If necessary, tell them that they can wear sun cream, sun-hats and sun-glasses, and sit in the shade.

Cover a display board with green backing paper. Paint strips of corrugated card to make tree trunks and branches, and staple them into position on the display. Organize the children into groups to make leaves for the trees. Glue pieces of green tissue paper in different shades onto leaf shapes. Mount them onto green backing paper and then staple to the branches of the trees. Cut leaf shapes from brown tissue paper and glue these beneath the trees to represent shade. Make a sun by gluing pieces of red and orange Cellophane to a circle of paper. Add rays made in the same way, then staple the completed sun into position.

If possible, take a group of children outside and use brown wax crayons on white paper to make rubbings of fence posts. Cut out the rubbings and staple to the display to make a fence. Create shade by painting shadows underneath the fence posts at an angle.

Draw an outline of a parasol and divide it into sections. Let the children fill alternate sections by gluing on scraps of yellow and red fabric. Decorate a rectangular piece of white paper with alternate squares of red and yellow to make a table-cloth. Staple the cloth to the bottom of the display, with the parasol at the side. Add a painted cardboard tube or strip of paper for a handle. Decorate four paper cups and plates and staple them into place on the cloth. Staple two pictures of children that the children have drawn or painted. Add an appropriate title.

Talk about
● Talk about the importance of

The sun can be dangerous

covering up on sunny days. Discuss the various things that we can do to keep ourselves safe.

● Familiarize the children with the places around your setting which provide shade.

Home links
● Ask parents and carers to reinforce the sun safety message.

● Organize a working party to create shady areas at the setting for example by planting trees, building shelters and creating a willow structure.

● Ask parents and carers to supply sun protection items for a table-top display. Make sure that sun cream bottles are empty. Also ask parents to provide sun-hats for their children on hot days.

Using the display
Personal, social and emotional development
● Organize a teddy bears' picnic. Let the children identify a suitable shady spot outside for the picnic.

Language and literacy
● Make a list of simple rules for playing in the sun. Scribe the children's ideas for them on individual sheets of paper and let the children illustrate them to make safety posters.

Mathematical development
● Look at the pattern of the picnic cloth. Notice how the squares fit together. What do you notice about the position of the colours? Look at horizontal, vertical and diagonal lines and talk about the patterns.
● Organize a teddy bears' picnic in the role-play area. How many plates, cups, spoons and so on will the children need to lay out for two teddy bears? How many for four teddy bears?

Knowledge and understanding of the world
● Let the children stand in the sun and look at their own shadows. What do they notice about their shadows at different times of the day?
● Find out about the science behind shadows by reading *My Shadow* in the *Simple Science* series (A & C Black).
● Look at the photocopiable sheet on page 76. Challenge the children to identify the different objects from their shadow shapes.
● Show the children a sundial and explain how to read the time using the position of the shadow. Compare a sundial with an analogue clock.

Physical development
● Let the children create shadow shapes using their bodies. Can they stand up tall to make a long, thin shadow? What about a star shape? Can they run away from their shadow? Find the best way to make a tiny or huge shadow.

Summer

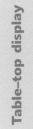

THEMES ON DISPLAY
for early years

Sun safety

Learning objective: to understand that we need to protect ourselves from the sun's harmful rays.

What you need
Cardboard boxes; rush beach mats; collection of sun protection items including parasol, sun-glasses, sun cream, sun-hats and long shorts brought in from home by the children; card; thick felt-tipped pen.

What to do
Prepare a table-top by arranging the cardboard boxes and covering the entire area with the rush beach mats.

Gather the children together and, one at a time, invite them to show the item they have brought in for the display. Encourage them to say why they have chosen the item. How does it keep them safe in the sun? Can they tell the other children when they used the item? Maybe it was on a recent holiday, or during the summer when they played in the garden. Invite each child to place his or her item on the table-top, adding your own items to complete the display if you wish.

Talk about
● Discuss how the items protect us from the sun. Remind the children of other things such as shady trees or buildings, which can help to protect us.
● Reinforce the reason why we need to protect ourselves, making the children aware of the dangers of sunburn.
● Talk about the weather in hot countries. Have any of the children been to a very hot country?

Home links
● Send a letter to parents and carers a week before you set up the display asking them to help their children find appropriate items for the display, and to help the children to understand what the items are used for.
● Make parents and carers aware that you are going to talk about the dangers of the sun so that they can support the topic sensitively at home.

Further display table ideas
● Make a display of items that people wear and use when they go swimming such as swimwear, goggles, hat, towel and armbands.
● Make a collection of toys and games equipment that the children play with in the summer such as tennis rackets and balls, paddling pool, play vehicles, buckets and spades. Include pictures of places that people visit, such as the park, the seaside or the swimming pool.
● Invite the children to bring in postcards, photographs, souvenirs, seaside rock and so on to create a colourful holiday display.

Autumn

Autumn colours

Learning objective: to learn about the changing colours of autumn.

What you need
Sugar paper and fabrics in autumn colours; autumn pictures; ribbon; white card; stapler, cardboard boxes; story, information and poetry books about autumn such as *Seasons Poems* compiled by John Foster (Oxford University Press), *Out and About Through the Year* by Shirley Hughes (Walker Books) or *Autumn* by Nicola Baxter (*Toppers* series, Watts Books); autumn items brought in by the children.

What to do
The day before you intend to create the display, cover a board with sugar paper in autumn colours. Drape fabrics around the board and intersperse with ribbon, pictures and rhymes about autumn. Make colour labels, double mounted on appropriately-coloured paper. Place cardboard boxes covered with autumn coloured paper in front of the board.

The next day, gather the children together in front of the display. Share the books and read some poems. Look at and talk about the colours of the paper and fabric on the display board. Invite the children to compare the colours on the display board with the colours of the trees and leaves in the pictures and books.

Tell the children that they are going to make a display about all the colours that they can see in autumn. Take them on a walk in and around your setting to look for natural and manufactured items in autumn colours. Pick up fallen leaves or conkers, collect wooden bricks or look for colourful fabrics. Add these to the covered cardboard boxes in front of the display. Invite the children who have brought items from home to add these to the appropriate boxes.

Talk about
● Talk about the changing colours of the leaves during autumn. What happens to the leaves after they have changed colour? Have any of the children ever walked through piles of leaves or helped to clear them up in the garden?

Home links
● Take the children outside your setting to look for autumn colours. Ask parents and carers to accompany you. Encourage them to continue the activity over a number of weeks, noticing the changing colours in the natural world.
● Write to parents and carers the week before you intend to create the display to ask them to help their children to find items such as fallen leaves, pictures and postcards of autumn colours, conkers and other fruits and seeds.

The changing colours of autumn provide the inspiration for this selection of vibrant displays. Ideas include creating a hedgerow full of berries, making handprint autumn animals and looking at ways to brighten up dark nights.

Autumn

Autumn leaves

Learning objective: to learn that some trees lose their leaves in autumn.

What you need
Green backing paper; sugar paper in autumn colours; white paper; paint in various colours; paintbrushes; corrugated card; lots of leaves in a variety of colours, shapes and sizes; bark rubbings; wax crayons; scissors; PVA glue and spreaders; stapler.

What to do
Talk to the children about what happens to the leaves on the trees during the autumn time. If possible, go outside and look at some trees around your setting. Are they still green? Are the leaves still on the trees or are they beginning to fall? What colours are they? Show the children your collection of fallen leaves. What colours can they see? Encourage them to describe the shapes, colours and textures of the leaves.

Cover a display board with green backing paper. Organize the children into groups. Show them how to paint the reverse of a leaf and then press it firmly onto a sheet of paper to make a leaf print, then let them make their own using a variety of colours of paint on white paper. When dry, cut them out and staple them in a repeating pattern around the edge of the display board.

Paint the corrugated card brown and staple to the board to make a tree trunk and branches. Attach the bark rubbings. Ask the children to paint some of the larger leaves with PVA glue. When dry, arrange the leaves around the bottom of the trunk and at the ends of the branches. Create more leaves by making wax rubbings on autumn coloured paper. Cut them out and attach them around the base of the tree trunk. Add an appropriate title to finish your display.

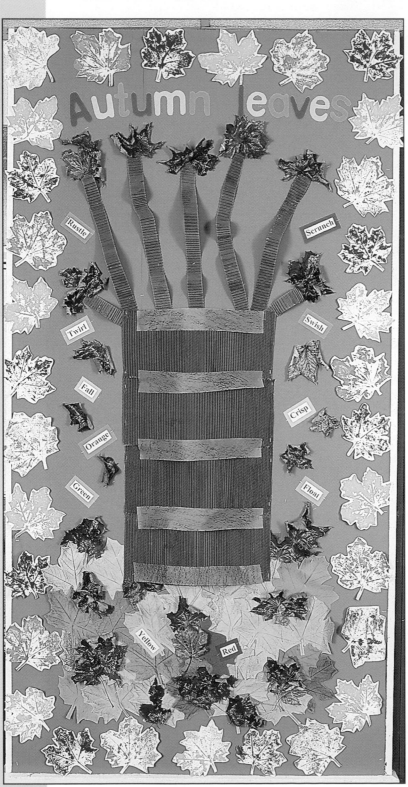

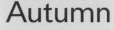

Using the display
Personal, social and emotional development
● Write a prayer with the children to thank God for the world that we live in. Ask the children to consider all the living things in the world that we have to be thankful for.

Language and literacy
● Develop language to describe the textures of the leaves such as scrunch, dry, crunchy, scratch, and the way in which they fall, such as twirl, swish or float. Make labels of the words and add them to the display.
● Write a group poem incorporating the children's descriptive words.
● Visit 'Infant Explorer' at www.naturegrid.org.uk

Mathematical development
● Look at the repeating pattern of colours around the border of your display. Provide coloured beads, blocks and counters and let the children make up their own repeating pattern using two and then three colours and objects.
● Sort the leaves into sets according to their size, shape and colour.

Knowledge and understanding of the world
● Use a paint program such as *Painter* (Windows) (Black Cat) on the computer to make pictures and patterns using the colours red, yellow, brown and orange.
● Talk about the trees that do not lose their leaves in the autumn.

Creative development
● Challenge the children to mix red and yellow paint to make shades of orange and brown for the leaf prints.
● Create a dance about falling leaves using either your own music or autumn music from *Seasons* published by Primrose Education Resources.

Talk about
● Take a look at the plants around your setting. Can the children see any flowers? What do they think has happened to them?
● Talk about the trees around your setting. Are they all losing their leaves? If it is a windy day, let the children watch the leaves being blown from the branches.

Home links
● Ask parents and carers to help with the leaf-printing activity.
● Organize a visit to a local park or woodland area to collect fallen leaves and ask parents and carers to help.

September

Learning objective: to learn that crops are harvested in September.

What you need

Display surface or boxes; yellow backing paper; red border; blue, black and green tissue paper; red paint; paintbrushes; paper; scissors; pinking shears; ears of corn; bread; flour; play cakes and rolls; cereal boxes; cereals and oats; bowls and baskets; harvest fruit; white card; black felt-tipped pen; PVA glue; spreaders; stapler; posters, pictures and books about harvest.

What to do

Cover a board with yellow backing paper. Staple blue tissue paper across the top of the board to make the sky and add a red border. If you wish, add a title to your display.

Gather the children together in front of the board and talk to them about harvest time. Explain that during the harvest, people gather in all the crops and store them for the winter. For example, some farmers cut their wheat, corn and other crops, and others gather apples, pears, plums and other fruit. Some vegetables such as potatoes, pumpkins and onions are dug up and stored away. Show the children the posters, pictures and books about harvest. Explain that it is also a time for people to think about others. Talk about harvest festivals, and explain that food is sometimes donated and then given to people in the community.

Tell the children that you are going to make a display to show that September is the beginning of harvest time.

Ask the children to make a poppy each. Invite them to paint red flower heads then, when dry, cut around them with pinking shears. Make the centres of the poppies from black tissue paper. Ask the children to cut a strip of green tissue paper (or felt) for the stalk.

With a small group of children, glue the corn to the yellow section of the

Using the display

Personal, social and emotional development

● Create a baker's shop in the role-play area. Let the children buy and sell a variety of wheat products.

Language and literacy

● Read the traditional story of 'The Little Red Hen'. Invite the children to paint pictures of different parts of the story and then provide a sentence for you to scribe on the pictures. Display the children's work around the room to make a wall frieze.
● Focus on the letter 's' by making an 's for September' display. Challenge the children to try to find things in and around your setting to add to the display.

Mathematical development

● Sing and act out the rhyme 'Five Currant Buns' from *This Little Puffin...* compiled by Elizabeth Matterson (Puffin) with the children.
● Use play money in the role-play baker's shop. Use 1p, 2p and 5p coins for younger children, and introduce 10p and 20p coins for older or more able children.
● Make a pictogram of the children's favourite cereal, cakes or bread.

Knowledge and understanding of the world

● Talk about how foods are harvested. Explain that some are picked and some are dug up either by hand or using special machines.
● Look at the cereal boxes and talk about the crops that the cereals are made from.
● Find out how bread is made by sharing an information book such as *Bread* in the *What's for Lunch?*' series (A & C Black).

Creative development

● Make items for the baker's shop from play dough.
● Learn the song about fruit and vegetables called 'Paintbox' from *Harlequin* (A & C Black).

---

board. Invite each child to stick their flower head and stalk among the corn.

Cover the display surface or cardboard boxes with yellow paper and arrange in front of the display. Display the bread, flour, cereal boxes and play food on the surface, and arrange some apples, pears or plums in a basket. Pour some flour or oats into a bowl for the children to touch and investigate. Ask the children for suggestions for labels, then write these onto white card and display with the appropriate items.

Talk about

● Talk about the corn. Look at the cereals and explain that many of these are made from corn. Tell the children that the corn is also ground up to make flour. What can they see on the display that is made from flour?

Home links

● Organize a baking session and invite parents and carers to come and help. Try making oat biscuits or simple bread rolls and loaves.

● Visit a local shop to look at the variety of breads on sale. Invite parents and carers to come with you.
● Write to parents and tell them what you intend to do. Ask them to save empty cereal boxes and bread wrappers.

Autumn

October

Learning objective: to learn that there are fewer hours of daylight during autumn and winter.

What you need
Dark blue backing paper; black sugar paper; paints; paintbrushes; tracing paper; gummed paper; white paper; templates of children, stars, cars and houses; white chalk; scissors; recyclable materials; PVA glue; spreaders; stapler; *Can't You Sleep, Little Bear?* by Martin Waddell and Barbara Firth (Walker Books).

What to do
Cover a display board with dark blue

backing paper and make a road and night sky from black sugar paper. Use chalk to add a white line down the centre of the road.

Read the story *Can't You Sleep, Little Bear?* to the children and talk about how it gets dark earlier during the autumn months. If relevant, talk about the clocks going back one hour. Talk about some of the ways that we light up our houses and towns when it gets dark. What do cars have that help drivers to see in the dark? What do we switch on at home when it gets dark in the evenings? Explain that you are going to make a display to show different forms of lighting.

Organize the children into small groups to make different parts of the display. Let one group draw around star templates, cut out the shapes and paint them yellow. When dry, glue into position on the dark sky. Let another group draw and cut out car outlines, then cover the shapes with gummed paper in their choice of colour. Staple the cars along the roadway. Add circles of yellow gummed paper to the front of each car for headlights and arrange strips set at angles to represent beams of light.

Invite the children to paint houses in a colour of their choice and, when dry, add illuminated windows made from yellow gummed paper. Staple these across the board. Attach squares of tracing paper in front to produce the effect of shadows. Add streetlights cut from black paper with beams of light cut from red gummed paper.

Let a small group paint outlines of children, making one for each house on the display. Staple these in front of each house and give a few of them torches cut from black paper with yellow beams of light.

Provide a range of recyclable materials and let the children make cars and other vehicles. Place these on the floor in front of the display. Finally, add a title to your display.

Talk about
● Talk about the dangers of electricity. Remind the children that they should never touch electrical plugs and switches without adult supervision.
● Talk about day and night. Let the

Using the display
Personal, social and emotional development
● Read the children a simple version of the story of 'The Creation' as told in the Bible (Genesis, Chapter 1).

Language and literacy
● Learn nursery rhymes about night-time, such as 'Twinkle, Twinkle, Little Star' and 'Wee Willie Winkie'.

Mathematical development
● Count the sides and points on the stars. Draw some more stars with different numbers of points. Make stars with five, six, seven or eight points. Talk about even and odd numbers of points.
● Talk with the children about the shapes used to make the houses. Count the number of sides and corners on a rectangle and square.
● Count the stars in the display. Alter the number daily and encourage the children to count to find how many stars there are each day.

Knowledge and understanding of the world
● Invite the children to watch as you take a torch apart. Identify and name the bulb, battery and switch, and demonstrate how to turn the torch on and off. Remind the children of the dangers of opening battery compartments and explain to them that they must not take objects apart at home.
● Collect and draw lots of different kinds of lights and lamps to make a table-top display.
● Talk about the things that give light naturally such as the sun, moon and stars and things that need power to make light.
● Find out how people used to light their homes years ago.

Creative development
● Paint light pictures on dark paper and dark pictures on light paper. Display the pictures around large silhouettes of the children cut from black sugar paper.

children draw pictures of some of the things that they do in the daytime, and the things that they do at night. What do the children notice?
● Talk about people who work at night such as delivery people, doctors, nurses and police officers. Why do these people need to work at night?

Home links
● Ask parents and carers to reinforce the dangers of electricity to the children at home.
● Invite parents and carers to contribute any items that they may have that would be appropriate to a display of different light sources.

The hedgerow

Learning objective: to find out about autumn fruits and berries.

What you need

Pale blue backing paper; green, yellow, orange and brown paint; sponges; paintbrushes; PVA glue and spreaders; oak leaf shapes and strips cut from corrugated card; acorns, conkers and other seeds; blackberries, rosehips and haws; purple, green and red tissue paper; lilac, green and red sugar paper; Blu-Tack; stapler.

What to do

Cover a display board with pale blue backing paper. Add grass made from spears of tissue paper and sugar paper painted in different shades of green.

If possible, take the children on a short walk around your setting or to a suitable local area to look at trees and hedgerows. Stress emphatically to the children that they must not pick or eat anything. Collect some leaves, nuts and cases that have fallen onto the ground yourself.

Back at your setting, look at and talk about the things that you have seen and

collected. Reinforce the safety message that the children should never eat anything that they find.

Look at blackberries, haws and rosehips and talk about where they grow. Tell the children that you would like them to help you make an autumn hedgerow display including some of the things that they saw on their walk.

Organize the children into two groups. Ask one group to paint corrugated card strips using brown paint and oak leaf shapes in green and orange. Staple the brown strips to make the tree trunk, branches and hedgerow. Glue the green leaves to the branches and the orange leaves on the grass. Sponge-paint another set of leaf shapes for the hedgerow.

Ask a second group to make blackberries and haws. Cut circles from lilac and red sugar paper and cover them with red and purple tissue paper using PVA glue. Let the children glue these onto the display.

Gather everyone in front of the display and together use glue and Blu-Tack to attach leaves, acorns, conkers and other things that you have collected to the display.

Talk about
● Discuss the colours of the berries. Ask the children to think of berries that we see at other times of year such as strawberries, raspberries and gooseberries.

● Talk about the dangers of eating things that we do not recognize, such as berries and nuts, which may be poisonous.
● Bring in a collection of boxes, wrappers and pictures of food made from autumn fruits and berries such as apple and blackberry pie, rosehip syrup and confectionery containing nuts. Check for allergies before letting the children handle any packaging.

Home links
● Invite parents and carers to accompany you on your walk around the setting and to help with the cooking activity.
● Tell parents and carers that you have been reinforcing the dangers of eating nuts and berries, and ask them to stress this to the children.
● Explain your display to parents and carers and ask for information about any allergies among the children.

Using the display
Personal, social and emotional development
● Talk about the importance of taking care of the environment, and how we should never pick things from plants in the wild.
● Find out about the birds and animals that live in the hedgerows and trees.

Mathematical development
● Count the acorns and conkers on the display.
● Use the conkers to make up number sentences. Move them around the display to make smaller sets that make five, for example.

Knowledge and understanding of the world
● Visit a supermarket to look at different berries and to find different products containing berries, fruit and nuts. The cereal and biscuit aisles are good for this activity.
● Invite parents and carers to come in and help the children to make blackberry and apple pie or crumble, and blueberry muffins.

Physical development
● Make berries and other fruit from play dough. Encourage the children to practise rolling small amounts between their hands and between their fingers and thumbs.

Autumn animals

Learning objective: to learn that some animals make special preparations for winter.

What you need
Green backing paper; sugar paper in autumn colours; wax crayons in autumn colours; leaves; leaf templates; scissors; template of a large squirrel and hedgehog; green Cellophane; brown, grey and black paint; PVA glue and spreaders; a selection of toy animals found mainly in autumn; cardboard boxes covered in autumn colours; stapler; information and story-books about animals that hibernate; the photocopiable sheet on page 77.

What to do
Cover a display board with green backing paper and add a title. Talk about animals that hibernate in the autumn. Look at information books and read stories such as *The Winter Hedgehog* by Ann and Reg Cartwright (Red Fox). Show the children the collection of leaves and explain that you are going to use these and the leaves created by the children to cover the board and make a cosy area for some autumn animals to snuggle into.

Show the children how to use the wax crayons to make leaf rubbings. Cut out the leaves and invite the children to glue them to the display to cover the entire area. Add texture by attaching leaves cut from green Cellophane and real leaves covered with PVA glue. Glue these on top of the leaf rubbings.

Make a hedgehog and squirrel. Organize the children to make lots of handprints using brown and grey paint. When dry, cut the handprints out and glue them to the squirrel and hedgehog templates, leaving the hedgehog's face to be painted. Paint on eyes and add features to the hedgehog.

Place the covered cardboard boxes in front of the display and put the models, pictures and books on top.

Talk about
● Talk about hibernation. Which animals gather food for winter? What do they gather? Where do they store it?
● What other animals hibernate? Talk about dormice, tortoises, bears and other animals that sleep through winter.

Home links
● Invite parents and carers to contribute to the display with books, pictures and models.
● Invite some adults to come into your setting to help with the cutting out of leaves and handprints.

Using the display
Personal, social and emotional development
● Explain how important it is to leave the countryside undisturbed, so that the animals can use the natural habitat to support their needs.
● Tell the children that they can help to keep hibernating animals safe during the autumn by leaving shed doors open and by leaving leafy areas undisturbed. Tell them also that sometimes, hibernating animals hide in piles of wood that are going to be used for bonfires, and to ask an adult to check before lighting them.

Language and literacy
● Develop pencil control skills by completing the hedgehog on the photocopiable sheet on page 77.
● Learn 'There's a Hedgehog on the Grass' from *This Little Puffin...* compiled by Elizabeth Matterson (Puffin).

Mathematical development
● Use handprints to measure items in your setting. How many handprints is a table? What about a bookcase? Make lists of things that are bigger and smaller than the children's hands.

Knowledge and understanding of the world
● Use a CD-ROM program to find out about creatures and their habitats or visit www.naturegrid.org.uk

Creative development
● Make up a poem or learn a song such as 'Which Animal?' from *Birds and Beasts* (A & C Black). Use percussion to add a simple accompaniment to depict different creatures. For example, scrapers and maracas are good for hedgehogs walking through dried leaves and undergrowth.
● Create a dance reflecting the movement of different animals.

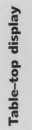

THEMES ON DISPLAY for early years

Autumn fruits and vegetables

Learning objective: to learn where some fruits and vegetables are grown, and which are safe to eat.

What you need
Fabric; baskets of different shapes and sizes; variety of fresh fruit and vegetables brought in by the children; white card; coloured card; black felt-tipped pen.

What to do
Cover a display surface with fabric and arrange the baskets across the top. Invite the children to group the fruits and vegetables and to place them into separate baskets or arrange them on the surface. Make labels for each of the fruit and vegetables and double mount them onto coloured card, folded in half so that they stand up.

Talk about
● Talk about the vegetables that are grown locally and those that come from other countries. Do the same for the fruits. Make two separate displays.
● Talk about the children's favourite fruits and vegetables from the display.

Are there any that they don't like? Why?

Home links
● Inform parents and carers about the display and invite them to contribute fruits and vegetables from their gardens if appropriate.
● Invite a gardener to come into your setting to talk about and show the children some of the things that he or she has grown.
● Look at some garden implements and talk about how each one is used.

Further display table ideas
● Make collections of items that are red, orange, green, brown and yellow and display these on separate colour tables. Organize colour weeks throughout autumn.
● Make a display of pictures, empty tins and boxes of food items that contain fruits and vegetables. Include soups, empty frozen food boxes and yoghurt pots, biscuit and sweet wrappers. Avoid nut products in case of allergies. Display the collection on a table covered in wallpaper with a vegetable and fruit design.
● Make a display of models and pictures of hedgehogs, squirrels and other animals usually seen out and about in autumn.

Winter

Cosy clothes

Learning objective: to understand that we wear warm clothes during winter.

What you need
Pale blue backing paper; black and neutral sugar paper; white netting or thin fabric; the photocopiable sheet on page 78; sponges; paints; paintbrushes; silver foil; white paper; winter clothing – a thick jumper, scarf, woolly hat, boots, winter coat, gloves and mittens; PVA glue; spreaders; scissors; stapler; story-book about winter such as *First Snow* by Kim Lewis (Walker Books).

What to do
Cover the board with pale blue backing paper and, using the template on page 78, invite a group of children to sponge-paint snowflakes using black sugar paper and white paint. Ruffle and staple white netting or fabric across the bottom of the board and attach snowflakes made from silver foil or hologram paper.

Read a story about winter such as *First Snow*. Look at the pictures in the book and talk about and name the clothes that the characters wear. Ask the children what they wear to go outside in the cold weather. Tell them that you are going to make a display that shows some warm winter clothes. Investigate the collection of clothing and tell the children that you would like them to help you dress three figures in the clothes.

Spread a sheet of neutral sugar paper on the floor and draw around three children. Cut out the outlines and let the children paint the skin tones and features. Staple to the board. Ask the children to choose clothes to dress the figures, including gloves, boots and hats. Add a title and labels for each item of clothing.

Talk about
● Discuss the order in which the children get dressed in the morning. What do they put on first? What do they put on last?

Home links
● Tell parents and carers about your display and ask them to let the children dress themselves in the morning.
● Ask parents and carers to contribute clothing that will fit a large teddy. Invite them to help the children dress the toys in your setting for a cold winter's day.
● Ask parents to contribute fasteners such as zips, Velcro, buttons, hooks, buckles and toggles for the children to practise their fastening skills.

From Advent trees to snowmen, the display ideas in this chapter will help children to understand about the sights, sounds and celebrations of winter.

Winter birds

Learning objective: to find out how we can help birds to survive during winter.

What you need
Green and pale blue backing paper; corrugated card; black sugar paper; paints; white spray paint; paintbrushes; blue, yellow, black, red and brown tissue paper; pictures of bird tables; nets containing nuts (check for allergies); the photocopiable sheet on page 79; recipe ingredients; bird templates; white paper; glue; stapler; books about birds.

What to do
Cover the bottom two thirds of the display board with green and the top of the board with pale blue backing paper. Talk about winter weather. Do the children like to go outside or stay inside when it is cold? Explain that animals try to find warm, dry places to shelter from the weather. Talk about the problems of finding food in the winter. Discuss the difficulties of digging for worms when the soil is frozen or looking for berries and fruit when the trees and bushes are empty. Explain that some animals collect and store food in autumn and this sees them through the winter, but birds cannot do this, so we can help by providing food for them.

Talk about different foods that birds like to eat. Look at the picture of the bird table and the net of nuts. In small groups, follow the recipe on the photocopiable sheet to make bird cakes,

While the bird cakes are setting, organize a group to paint strips of corrugated card to make fence posts. Staple these across the bottom of the board. Make two bird tables from corrugated card and mount these on the display. Suspend nets of nuts and the children's bird cakes from them.

Make some birds using different techniques. Provide templates and invite the children to use paint or collage to make blue tits, blackbirds, starlings, robins, crows or sparrows. Staple the birds around the display.

Add a title to complete the display. Arrange a selection of books and pictures in front of the display and add some bird cake ingredients and completed bird cakes. Making sure that the children are at a safe

Using the display

Personal, social and emotional development

● Talk about the importance of leaving the birds alone when they are feeding. Remind the children that they must not frighten the birds.
● Think about the needs of other animals in wintertime. Discuss the problems of frozen water, frozen soil and snow-covered trees.
● Learn the hymn 'Little Birds in Wintertime' from *Someone's Singing Lord* (A & C Black).

Language and literacy

● Learn rhymes and songs about birds such as 'Little Robin Redbreast' or 'Two Little Blackbirds' from *This Little Puffin...* compiled by Elizabeth Matterson (Puffin) or 'The North Wind Doth Blow' from *Sing Hey Diddle Diddle* (A & C Black).
● Look at information books about birds and find the birds in your display. Scribe short sentences using the children's suggested text.

Mathematical development

● Count the number of robins, starlings and blackbirds in the display.
● Develop positional language by attaching a bird to the display using Blu-Tack. Encourage the children to move it around the display – place it on the fence, under the bird table, next to a robin and so on.

Knowledge and understanding of the world

● Set up a bird feeder near to a window. Over a number of days, count the birds that visit. What type of bird visited most frequently?
● Talk to the children about the hot countries that the birds fly to. Find these on a globe.

Creative development

● Create a dance to show the different ways that birds move. Include the birds' disappointment when they cannot dig up worms in the soil, and their delight at finding food on a bird table.

distance, spray parts of the display with white spray paint to represent frost.

Talk about

● Talk about the birds that do not stay in this country during the winter months, introducing the word 'migrate'. Why do these birds fly south? Explain that they fly to warmer countries where there is a plentiful supply of food.
● Talk about when to stop feeding the birds. Explain that small nuts and seeds can be harmful to baby birds, and so we should stop feeding the birds in the spring.

Home links

● Invite parents to help the children to make the bird cake.
● Ask parents and carers to take their children to appropriate places to see and feed local birdlife such as ducks, seagulls or pigeons.

THEMES ON DISPLAY
for early years

Christmas Advent tree

Learning objective: to count the days to Christmas during December.

What you need
Story about the Nativity such as *The First Christmas* by Georgie Adams and Anna Leplar (Dolphin); red and green paper; drawing and colouring materials; scissors; stapler; 25 white paper circles; small Christmas tree templates; sponges; green and yellow paint; 25 small tree decorations or sweets; thread; Christmas tree; decorations; Advent calendars and candles; tinsel.

What to do
Cover a display board with red backing paper. Read and discuss the story of the Nativity with the children. Talk about the children's own experiences of Christmas. How do they count down the days to Christmas? Introduce the Advent calendars and candles and, together, open the doors of the calendars or count the days on the candle. Explain that you would like the children to help you make an Advent tree to count down the days until Christmas.

Cut a large Christmas tree shape from green paper and staple it to the board. Number the white paper circles from 1 to 25 and staple them randomly to the tree. Tie a piece of thread around each of the 25 tree decorations or sweets and suspend one next to each number. Decorate around the edge of the tree with tinsel.

Organize the children into small groups to sponge-paint Christmas trees for a border using the tree templates. Encourage them to add a yellow star at the top of their tree once the green paint has dried.

Make a title with letters cut from brightly-coloured paper and suspended

Using the display
Personal, social and emotional development
● Find out about other festivals that happen during wintertime, such as Hanukah, Ramadan and Ganjitsu. Find out about the stories behind the festivals.

Language and literacy
● Hold your own simple Nativity play, encouraging the children to re-enact the story of the birth of Jesus using toy props.

Mathematical development
● Talk about the numbers in the Nativity story. How many Wise Men were there? How many presents did they bring? How many presents would there be if the Wise Men each brought two?
● Each day, start from number one and count up to the appropriate number.

Knowledge and understanding of the world
● Find out how people celebrate Christmas in other countries.
● Talk about how Christmas gifts have changed over the years. If possible, compare some gifts that might have been given years ago, such as oranges, wooden toys and teddy bears with some gifts that the children may receive now.

Physical development
● Provide objects in a variety of shapes for the children to wrap. Organize additional adult help for this.

Creative development
● Make papier mâché Christmas trees or decorations. Paint them with bright colours and add sequins or glitter.
● Learn some Christmas songs and carols. Provide a range of percussion instruments for the children to accompany the songs.

from tinsel across the display. Put up a Christmas tree nearby and let the children decorate it. Arrange table decorations and candles on a display surface.

During the Advent season, invite one child each day to find the correct number on the display. Take down the present or sweet associated with that day and let the child add it to the decorated Christmas tree nearby.

Talk about
● Discuss the meaning of Advent. Explain to the children that it is the time before the coming of Christ. Tell them that the word Christmas comes from the word Christ.
● Share the children's experiences of Christmas. Discuss how this is a time for families and friends to get together and celebrate this special time.

Home links
● Organize a few adults to help with the painting of the Christmas trees for the border.
● Ask parents and carers to let the children bring in an item to add to a festive table-top display.

● Ask parents and carers to open an Advent calendar at home with the children and talk about the pictures behind the doors.

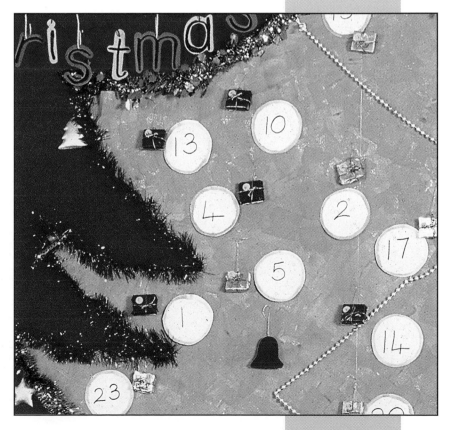

January snow

Learning objective: to learn that it sometimes snows in January.

What you need

Blue backing paper; paints; newspaper; cold-water paste (insect repellent-free); white, black and blue paper; two balloons or old large balls; chicken wire; two plastic carrots or orange paper cones; black buttons; white fabric, cotton wool or fire resistant furniture stuffing; stapler; the photocopiable sheets on pages 78 and 80; glitter; sponges; *The Snowman* by Raymond Briggs (Puffin); labels.

What to do

Cover a display board with blue backing paper. Place a table in front of the board and drape white fabric, cotton wool or fleecy furniture stuffing across the bottom of the board and the table-top. Blow up two balloons for the heads of the snowmen and mould chicken wire into body shapes.

Gather the children together and read them the story of *The Snowman* by Raymond Briggs. What happens to the snowman when it begins to get warm? How many of the children have seen snow? Can they remember how it feels? Ask them to describe how it feels if they are able and make a list of their suggestions.

Explain to the children that you are going to make a snowman display to show that sometimes in January we get snow. Show them the balloons and chicken wire shapes and demonstrate how to cover the surface with paste and strips of newspaper. Explain to the children that as the newspaper dries, it will harden.

Organize the children into four groups to glue several layers of newspaper to the shapes. Use white paper for the final layer and then join the heads to the bodies with several long strips to make the snowmen shapes. Leave to dry for several days. (If you do this part of the display on Friday, the sculptures will be dry by Monday morning.)

When completely dry, let the children help to paint the snowmen white. Either paint on the features or use buttons or coloured paper. Stick on plastic carrots or cones of orange paper for the noses. Place the snowmen models on the display.

Photocopy the snowflake template on page 78, enlarging or reducing it to make patterns of different sizes. Glue the shapes to the background to make a snowy sky.

Finish the display with a border made from the children's snowmen pictures. Use the stencil on page 80, and invite the children to

Using the display

Language and literacy
● Rewrite the story of *The Snowman* during a group activity.
● Write a class snowman poem.
● Learn the rhymes 'Who Made the Footprints in the Snow?' and 'A Chubby Little Snowman' from *This Little Puffin...* compiled by Elizabeth Matterson (Puffin).

Mathematical development
● Look at the shape of the snowflakes. Count the points. Fold paper circles into sixths and cut snowflakes with six points.
● Make paper cones with the children. Develop these into objects and models such as ice-cream cones, hats and mice. How many ideas can the children think of?
● Learn the counting rhyme 'Five Jolly Snowmen' in *Christmas Tinderbox* (A & C Black).

Knowledge and understanding of the world
● Look at other things that melt when they are heated such as butter and chocolate. Follow your setting's safety policy, and use a microwave, rather than hot water to melt items.
● Talk about other things that people do in the snow such as having snowball fights, sledding or skiing.

Physical development
● Make models of snowmen using a range of construction and malleable materials.

Creative development
● Pretend to be a snowman. Develop a movement piece to suitable music that follows the movements of the snowman as it melts in the sun.
● Use fabric and collage scraps to design a hat and scarf for a snowman. Choose shiny buttons for his coat.

sponge-paint the snowmen before adding features and hats, and then adding a sprinkling of glitter. Make labels of the children's suggested words and add these to the display and the table-top. Add a title such as 'January brings the snow'.

Talk about
● Discuss how the snow feels. If it has not snowed recently, use the 'snow' created around the freezer box in a refrigerator. Invite the children to describe what the snow feels like using both words and actions.
● Talk about the word 'freezing'. Explain that this is when the temperature drops below 0° Celsius.

Home links
● Send a letter to parents and carers asking them to build snowmen with their children if it snows!
● Ask at least four adults to help make the papier mâché snowmen with the children. Those that are unable to come into the setting could cut out some snowflake patterns at home.
● Ask parents and carers to contribute any appropriate fabrics and wools that they may have.

Frosty weather

Learning objective: to learn that February is a month for frosty weather.

What you need
Coloured backing paper; fabric in the same colour as the backing paper; white chalk; cotton wool; paint in a range of colours; paper; pens; wool; selection of fabrics including woolly jumpers cut into squares, offcuts of synthetic leather and lurex materials; PVA glue; spreaders; corrugated card; a copy of the song 'Here We Go Round the Mulberry Bush'; stapler; scissors; collection of cold weather clothes including hats, scarves, gloves, mittens and boots.

What to do
Cover a display board with backing paper. Place a display surface in front of the board and cover with fabric in the same colour as the backing paper. Use chalk and cotton wool to represent snow across the bottom of the board and on the display surface.

Sing the song 'Here We Go Round the Mulberry Bush' with the children. Invite them to suggest actions for other verses. For example, 'This is the way we keep our hands warm' and 'This is the way we wrap up warm'. Talk about frosty weather. What do we see when the weather is frosty?

Tell the children that you are going to make a picture of them dancing around a mulberry bush. What does a mulberry bush look like in winter? Does it have leaves or berries? Explain that, in the month of February, the bush will have bare branches with perhaps a little bit of frost on each one.

Invite the children to paint pictures of themselves using appropriate colours. When dry, help the children to cut out their pictures then invite them to use collage materials to make some warm clothing. Use woollen squares for jumpers, synthetic leather for boots and a range of fabrics for trousers, gloves and hats. Staple the figures to the display board. Staple strips of brown painted corrugated card to the centre of the board to make the mulberry bush. Use chalk to give the trunk and branches a frosty effect.

Write the verses and chorus of the song on a large sheet of paper in large writing or type them on a computer and print them out. Invite a small group of children to add illustrations around the text. Attach to the display. Arrange your collection of warm clothes in front of the display. Finally, add the title 'Frosty weather' to complete the display.

Talk about
● Talk about the times of day when we usually see frost – the morning, evening and night-time. Unless it is a very cold day, the frost has usually disappeared by lunch-time.

Home links
● Ask parents and carers to look out for signs of frost with their children during their journey to your setting. Provide a list of useful words to use to help widen the children's vocabulary.
● Ask parents and carers to freeze things at home and to talk about what they feel and look like. Invite them to write down the children's words to make a word list for the display.

Using the display
Personal, social and emotional development
● Talk about the clothes that the children wear when they play outside in the cold weather. What do they wear on their hands, feet and heads? What do they wear around their neck?
● Play some games to practise putting on and taking off winter clothes. Can the children do up their own buttons? Can they undo the zip on a coat?

Language and literacy
● Investigate words associated with frosty weather such as icy, glittering, shivery and so on. Make a list then use to make up a group poem.
● Talk about foods that are frozen.

Discuss and identify foods that are eaten frozen, such as ice-cream and lollies, and foods that we need to defrost, such as vegetables and bread.

Knowledge and understanding of the world
● Investigate freezing a range of solids and liquids. Remove items from the freezer section of a fridge and notice the frosting on the outside. What does it look like? What does it feel like?
● Make ice lollies in different flavours. (Check for allergies first.)

Creative development
● Make frosty pictures by sprinkling glitter onto glue outlines.
● Use icing sugar dissolved in water to paint frosty pictures on black or dark blue paper.

THEMES ON DISPLAY
for early years

Snowdrops

Learning objective: to learn about flowers that bloom in winter.

What you need
Blue and green backing paper; black, green and white sugar paper; Cellophane paper in various colours; dark and light green tissue paper; paints; paintbrushes; snowdrop bulbs, bulb fibre and a bowl; PVA glue and spreaders; scissors; stapler.

What to do
In October, plant snowdrop bulbs with the children. Include the activity with the planting of other indoor bulbs.

Make your display when the bulbs have flowered. Show them to the children and explain that snowdrops are often the first flowers to appear at the end of winter. If the bulbs fail to grow, use pictures of snowdrops instead. Explain that you are going to make a display to show how pretty the snowdrops look in the middle of winter.

Using the display

Personal, social and emotional development

● Remind the children that they must never pick any of the flowers that they find in the wild.

Language and literacy

● Find and label objects around your setting beginning with the letter 's'. Make a list of seasonal words beginning with 's' such as spring, shivery, snowy, slushy and so on.
● Invite the children to help you find other flowers that are made up of two words such as bluebell, sunflower and buttercup. Why do the flowers have these names?

Knowledge and understanding of the world

● Talk about the signs that the seasons are changing. What other signs can we see at this time of year that tell us that spring is on the way? Talk about baby animals, longer days, warmer weather and so on.
● Plant bulbs both indoors in pots and outside during October. Include crocuses, daffodils, hyacinths and snowdrops. Compare the bulbs grown inside with those grown outside.

Creative development

● Make winter trees by blowing brown paint through straws onto black paper. When dry, add clusters of snowdrops.

Cover a display board with blue and green backing paper to make the sky and grass. Invite the children to cut and glue triangles of dark and light green tissue paper to make the grass on the bottom half. Cut a church shape from black sugar paper and cut out sections to make windows. Glue squares of coloured Cellophane paper to the underside of the holes to make stained glass windows, then add painted paper frames to the front before stapling the church to the centre of the board. Paint a path leading to the door of the church.

Demonstrate how to cut three pointed oval shapes from white paper and glue them together to make a snowdrop. Glue them among the grass in clusters. Add a title to your display if you wish.

Talk about

● Why are these flowers called snowdrops? Look for clues in the colour and shape of the snowdrops.
● Talk about other early flowers such as crocuses and daffodils.
● Discuss the size of the flowers. Tell the children that snowdrops usually grow in clumps or groups. Can they suggest why this might be?

Home links

● Ask parents and carers to look for snowdrops in their gardens or on their journey to your setting and examine them carefully with their children.

● Organize for one or two additional adults to help make the snowdrops with the children.
● Ask parents and carers to help their children grow snowdrops and other winter flowers from bulbs at home.

Winter fabrics

Learning objective: to learn that winter clothes are made from warm materials.

What you need
Coloured paper or fabric; a collection of winter clothing including thick and waterproof coats, gloves and hats made from a variety of materials for both summer and winter wear; boots lined with warm fabric; thinner items such as T-shirts, dresses and socks; white card; black felt-tipped pen; cardboard boxes.

What to do
Arrange the cardboard boxes along the display surface and cover with coloured paper or fabric. Gather the children around the collection of clothing. Ask a child to choose one item from the collection, to feel it and pass it around the circle. As the item is being passed around, invite the children to say something about it. Is the material thick or thin? Fleecy or smooth? Would they wear the item in cold or warm weather? Repeat with each item.

When each item has been around the circle, place it into the centre of the circle in one of three piles: winter clothes; summer clothes; clothes for both seasons. Display the winter clothes on the prepared surface. Write labels with the children to describe the material and properties of each one. Decide together which items can be worn in summer and winter, and include these items. Discard the summer items.

Talk about
● Investigate the differences between the winter and summer clothes.
● Why do we wear wellingtons and not flip-flops, in winter? Find out why we do not wear other items such as sun-hats, swimming costumes, shorts and so on.

Home links
● Ask parents and carers to contribute items of clothing that the children no longer wear. Encourage them to donate distinctive items such as plastic raincoats, coats with hoods and so on.

Further display table ideas
● Cover a display surface with white fabric and display a collection of white items. Use white paint, wool and papers to make individual pictures and patterns to add to the display,
● Display a collection of silver objects and pictures to depict frost.
● Display a collection of wrapping paper, boxes, ribbons and bows used to wrap presents at Christmas.

Seasons

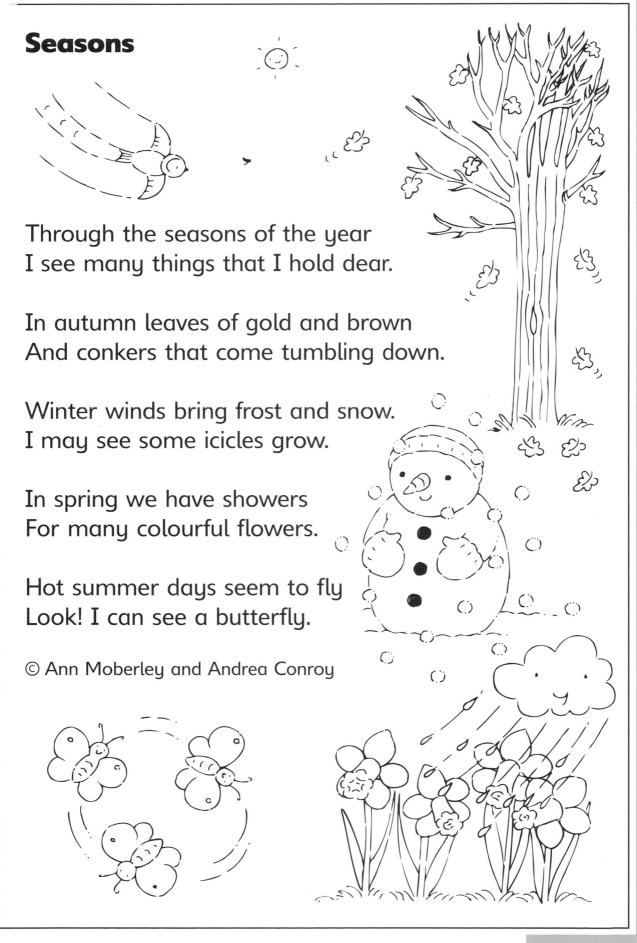

Through the seasons of the year
I see many things that I hold dear.

In autumn leaves of gold and brown
And conkers that come tumbling down.

Winter winds bring frost and snow.
I may see some icicles grow.

In spring we have showers
For many colourful flowers.

Hot summer days seem to fly
Look! I can see a butterfly.

© Ann Moberley and Andrea Conroy

Easter egg patterns

Trace the patterns in coloured pens or pencils to make an Easter egg picture.

Shape matching

Draw lines to match the shapes.
Colour the rectangles red, the circles yellow, the squares green and the triangles blue.

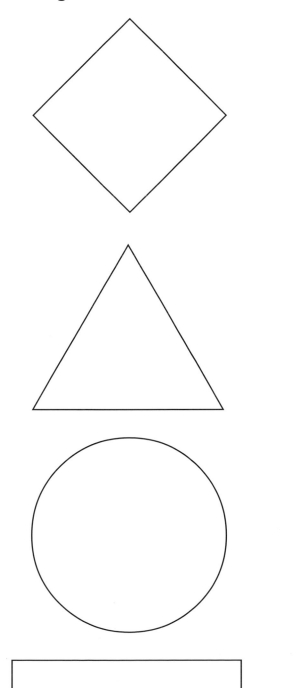
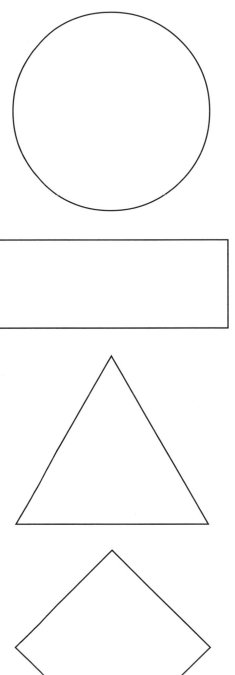

Photocopiable

Shadow pictures

Work out what the objects are from their shadows.

Hedgehog spines

Join up the dots to make the hedgehog's spines.
Colour the hedgehog brown.

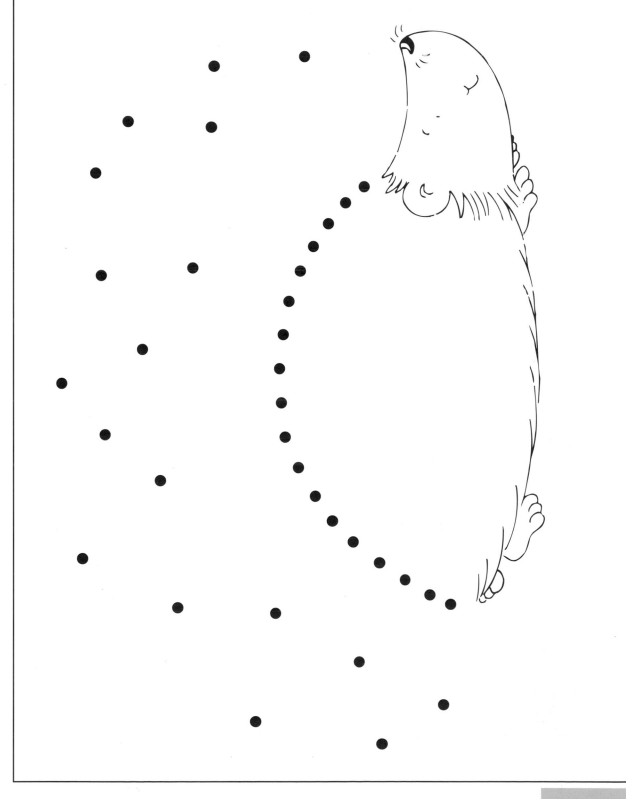

Snowflake

Bird cake recipe

What you need
- a handful of nuts
- several slices or crusts of bread
- 500g of lard
- a selection of seeds suitable for birds
- a length of string

What to do
- Melt the fat and allow to cool.
- Break up the bread into small pieces and mix with the seeds and nuts.
- Stir in the cool fat.
- Place a length of string inside the mixture.
- Put small amounts of the mixture into a foil mould and leave to set.
- Turn out the cake and tie the string around a tree branch.

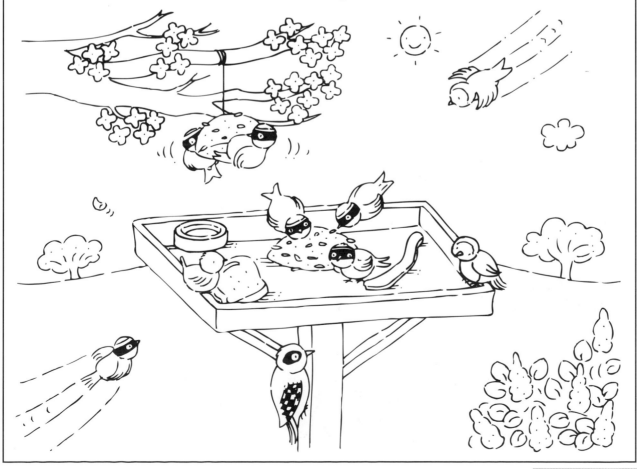

The snowman

SEASONS